MANAGING BY NEGOTIATIONS

MANAGING BY NEGOTIATIONS

Earl Brooks
and
George S. Odiorne

 VAN NOSTRAND REINHOLD COMPANY

Copyright © 1984 by Van Nostrand Reinhold Company Inc.

Library of Congress Catalog Card Number: 83-23407
ISBN: 0-442-20962-2

Manufactured in the United States of America

Published by Van Nostrand Reinhold Company Inc.
135 West 50th Street
New York, New York 10020

Van Nostrand Reinhold Company Limited
Molly Millars Lane
Wokingham, Berkshire RG11 2PY, England

Van Nostrand Reinhold
480 Latrobe Street
Melbourne, Victoria 3000, Australia

Macmillan of Canada
Division of Gage Publishing Limited
164 Commander Boulevard
Agincourt, Ontario M1S 3C7, Canada

15 14 13 12 11 10 9 8 7 6 5 4 3

Library of Congress Cataloging in Publication Data

Brooks, Earl.
  Managing by negotiations.

  Includes index.
  1. Negotiation in business.   I. Odiorne, George S.
II. Title.
HD58.6.B76   1984   658.4   83-23407
ISBN 0-442-20962-2

Preface

Negotiation used to be something that happened when labor met management or when two ambassadors from different countries met to wind up a war or forge a treaty. No longer. Now, everybody negotiates. Bosses negotiate objectives with their subordinates rather than simply tell them "do this or else." Tenants negotiate with landlords over maintenance and garbage pick up. Students negotiate with possible employers. Government contractors negotiate with bureaucrats and generals. In the modern home, kids often feel they have a right to negotiate with parents the rules of the house, their allowance, and their dress. In the eighties, we find that one and all think they have a right to be heard in those decisions that affect them, the unexplained directive being viewed with the enthusiasm displayed for ants at a picnic. We simply don't want other people telling us what to do, and we in turn tend to grant that we should talk things out with others as well.

This book suggests that most of us could do an even better job at negotiating in these many areas. Part I focuses upon some failures in management when negotiation skills were still in short supply. Negotiation, we suggest, is part of a new management style for the nineties, which all of us should study, cultivate, and polish. Yet, this skill doesn't consist of a simple set of check list routines to be followed slavishly. Rather, it starts with an assessment of your own personal strategy for negotiation, which will then become the building block of all your negotiating.

Part II draws upon the research of behavioral scientists and relates it to practical situations where negotiation is called for. The best approach is to seek unity and agreement that satisfies both sides, but this doesn't mean that anyone should enter negotiations with a pushover mentality. You go after what you want skillfully and vigorously, and so does the other side. In this way it is possible to find a sensible and satisfactory middle ground. You use power if you have it, you persuade, you are aggressive when it is called for—remembering all the while that you are willing to bend and give as well as take. This book discusses the tactics for dealing with equals or betters and also for dealing with a weak position. It spells out a unique four-part formula for negotiation and explains how each of them fits into a productive negotiation strategy. Sometimes you bargain alone; other times you bargain as part of a team. Your top management can be of help as a back-up. The final chapter includes some games and cases you can use to train yourself and others to apply the ideas proposed.

A word about the language and style of this book. There are many excellent theoretical as well as research-based books on the "science" of negotiations, but these are usually written for other theoreticians or researchers and not for general readers or managers and others in the swirling, complex world of business. The principles presented in this book have been drawn from the best research, but the language is geared to the operating professional. You'll find copious anecdotes and examples. Such an approach isn't scientific, of course, but it suits our purpose of teaching the reader *how* to negotiate, not of expounding a theory of negotiation. A book can serve as a wonderful teaching tool, and that's the real purpose here. The best way to use this book is to read it carefully, do the exercises, and rate yourself with the check lists. Think of this as a kind of self-development program. If your negotiation skills improve, we'll have achieved our objective.

Our deep thanks goes to a generation of students at Cornell and elsewhere who have studied negotiations under the authors. Appreciation is also expressed to Elaine Fydenkevez, who typed the final text, and to our wives, who were of inestimable help during the writing.

EARL BROOKS
GEORGE S. ODIORNE

Contents

MANAGING BY NEGOTIATIONS

PART I
A NEW MANAGEMENT
STYLE FOR THE NINETIES

During the 1970s, negotiations became a subject of interest to millions of people who had previously never thought of themselves as negotiators. Prior to this revolution, negotiations was something limited to a few specially trained and narrowly focused specialists such as labor relations experts, foreign service officers, or purchasing agents. During the seventies, everyone suddenly seemed to catch on that negotiations is something we all do daily, and our skill at it is an important part of the fabric of living.

The reason for this expansion of negotiations to cover life in general, and every facet of life in the world of work, can be explained by a change in the attitudes of people about their rights at work. People learned to expect that their opinions and interests would be sought out by managers and bosses, and that if somebody had an interest or a need, it should be expressed honestly and forcefully. Children expect parents to hear their side of the story, subordinates expect bosses to listen to their views, and private citizens stridently claim the right to talk to their government leaders and be listened to, and their needs attended to.

In short, more than a narrow technique, negotiations become an important new general-use tool of social relations for people in every walk of life. Part I of this book examines that new style of life and its major dimensions.

1
The Age of Negotiation

A MANAGERIAL STYLE FOR THE NINETIES

A couple of years ago a large grocery products company in the East decided to change its advertising media from mainly radio spots to television. One minor stumbling block was what to do about a long-term contract with a woman who had been featured in radio commercials, but whose presence in visual ads would be somewhat less than compelling. Since the ads stressed the modern health-building benefits of the food products she was selling, it seemed that her personal appearance would be an embarrassment. She weighed over 200 pounds. One wag described her as a "portly hamster." While her resonant and cool selling voice was a distinct selling advantage on radio, her more than corpulent appearance on the tube urging the masses to "keep slim with ABC's health products" would be ludicrous.

It was decided that she should be talked into an early retirement, and in order to make sure things were done just right, the group vice president of the consumer group announced that he would personally meet with her and renegotiate her contract. The contract unfortunately had just been rewritten eighteen months earlier and extended for seven years, with annual sweeteners, with the total dollars running into a high six figures over the life of the contract.

Thus one morning the vice president stuffed a few papers into his attaché case, hopped a plane, and headed out to resolve this minor matter. As occurs with so many executives who negotiate, things didn't work out exactly as everyone had hoped. When he returned, the staff found that he had given away the following concessions:

1. Ms. Puffy was not only to serve out the life of the contract, but an option to renew for another five years had been added.

2. Some fairly expensive side conditions had been added which sweet-

3

ened the package for Ms. Puffy by another $150,000 over the life of the contract.

3. Ms. Puffy would have exclusive rights to do the "voice over" for all TV commercials, and all personal appearances would be made by actresses whose form and face were more attuned to the slim image of the product advertising strategy.

4. Ms. Puffy further has the right to approve or veto the actresses chosen, and the chosen actresses would furthermore report to her.

5. The advertising agency was to obtain approval for all live sequences from Ms. Puffy before they were made.

6. In order to manage this entire new setup, Ms. Puffy was to be provided with added staff support and secretarial help, plus a more generous travel and expense budget.

As one wry observer back in corporate headquarters remarked: "She took everything but his shorts, and that's only because she didn't think they would fit her."

While the story is an extreme one, it is both true and all too typical of what can occur when a traditional executive drifts blindly into the negotiation process with a skilled negotiator. Puffy had followed all of the rules which modern negotiation theory and practice teach us, and the vice president was totally innocent of such lowly talents. The story could be duplicated again and again.

- New York City nearly gained the distinction of being the first major city to go bankrupt because the municipal employees unions under Victor Gotbaum were skilled negotiators, and the good mayor was their easy victim.
- Many a merger which would have led to a happy marriage for the two firms, their employees, and their stockholders collapsed because the negotiator for one side or another ripped the relationship to shreds before it was fairly started.
- During the seventies and early eighties a whole rash of company presidents took charge of companies as chief executive officer, only to be fired after six months to a year because the initial deal had been ineptly negotiated. At Ford, Dictaphone, CBS, Coca-Cola, ITT, and a host of other giant firms, the executive search among numerous outsiders, produced a top-flight candidate for the top spot, only to prove a disaster after he was aboard. Somewhere in the negotiations on the new assignment, the parties had missed some important elements of the negotiation process.

- In high-technology business, it was common during the seventies for whole teams of top-flight scientists to pack their bags and move over to a competitor, taking the entire strategic brains of the business with them, often because the former employer had botched the process of negotiating major grievances over their role and function in the firm.
- One large computer firm situated an important facility in an isolated city in northern New England and went about recruiting talented young people from leading colleges for key positions in finance, marketing, and engineering. Within two years ninety percent of those hired with such high expectations had left. Failing to negotiate with honesty and candor, the firm had overstated the benefits of the location and understated the cultural disadvantages; they had negotiated their way into an embarrassing impasse for the new division.

Examples like these are occurring every day, as inept negotiators fly in the face of changed expectations of people about their relationships to their employer, their colleagues, and their competitors.

THE END OF POWER-BASED MANAGEMENT

The coming of the eighties has seen a generation of workers, managers, and staff people who have greatly different expectations for their lives than prior generations. A generation of top management which was weaned in a world where bosses had power now expect that their interests and viewpoints will be listened to and accommodated, and they have moved into key positions in major organizations.

The old-fashioned manager negotiated in a crude kind of way, but on a single power basis. As one foreman in a big-city factory told us: "Sure I negotiate. They can do what I say and be damn quick about it or otherwise go someplace else." This honest statement of a bargaining position is a rough sort of negotiation. It gives the subordinate two choices, and the freedom to pick one or the other. The boss presents the options, and the decision is left to the subordinate. It is somewhat like the story told by Albert Camus of a German officer who informed a French mother that he intended to have one of her two sons shot for underground resistance, and she could choose which one! In today's age of negotiations, other forms of negotiation besides power have emerged in human relationships at the workplace. It's true that power still exists and is used, openly or covertly, but further bases of negotiation are now required. Here are fifteen reasons why power-based negotiations of the old-fashioned sorts are no longer sufficient.

1. *Leaders have been made to feel guilty* about the spotlight of wielding power. It has been drilled into us in school from the earliest years, and is fairly well embedded in modern culture, that the power seeker and power wielder is somehow a bad person.

2. *People in charge who will sometimes compromise* and perhaps even occasionally submit to others are considered somehow nobler and wiser than those who dominate, intimidate, coerce, and control others.

3. *Democracy and egalitarianism,* which have been the ideals of our political system, are now considered both ideal and attainable for the work place as well, and bosses are supposed to recognize this fact. Those who don't—and a goodly number do not—are somehow considered to be anathema. People should be able to choose their own acts.

4. *The revolution of the left-behinds,* including such people as women, racial minorities, ethnic groups, handicapped, ex-convicts, and those of alternative sex preferences, has stressed the need to talk to such people and learn of their interests and respond to their rights and needs. Such negotiation is often provided in laws of affirmative action, equal rights, and compensatory quotas.

5. *It is better to be interdependent than independent.* The prevailing culture which has emerged in the sixties and seventies makes it clear that we all need one another. Thus we should learn to encounter, confront, debate, and negotiate with one another in order that everyone gets in the act of sharing in the fruits of a modern society.

6. *Violence and terrorism are inferior* to discussion, debate, and civility in human relations. We view with horror and dismay the practices of the PLO, the IRA, or the Red Brigade. The right-thinking people of the world all admonish such groups to desist from such ruffianlike behavior and sit down and negotiate their way to their goal.

7. *Bureaucracy and complex forms of organization* produce a dehumanizing environment, and the people who are turned into instruments of organizations have a right to assert their individual rights and interests within that framework.

8. *People who are skilled in negotiation,* mediation, and conciliation are seen as having greater qualities of leadership than the brute who grows in power and then uses that power to grow more. The seeking of raw power is an almost automatic signal to the large masses of people

to turn against that leader and supplant him or her with another of more democratic leanings.

9. *Leaders are people who rule by the assent of the governed,* not people who seize power and wield it. The university president who fails to confer with the faculty, the corporate président who doesn't consider the interests of the various stakeholders, such as customers, stockholders, employees, and government regulators, are regularly unseated by their constituencies. This has produced a great turnover of leaders in the past decade at every level of society.

10. *Power has not been destroyed* by the coming of the age of negotiations, it has simply been spread more thinly among more people, rather than concentrated in the traditional leaders. This diffusion and fractionalizing of power is seen by people as being desirable, even if we sometimes pay for it in lower efficiency and higher costs.

11. *The rights of property* have been watered down in favor of the rights of the people. Horace Mann in 1842 asserted that "the great majority always have been and probably always will be comparatively poor, while a relative few will possess the greatest share of the world's goods." This idea went undisputed when Mann wrote it. Today the teachers' unions, legislators who listen to those unions, and parents who send their kids to the schools would all shout down Mann as an archaic monster. Negotiations today often center upon the achievement of equality, not only in pay and wealth, but in decision-making which affects people in their jobs, their homes, and their lives.

12. *There is little exuberance or excitement* over the way power is wielded these days, only the frustrations, the pains, the delays, and the inefficiencies of letting everyone join the decision-making process through negotiation.

13. *Garnering power is paid for by a whole series of small debts,* and these debts are paid in giving something to the governed. The process by which these debts are totted up and dispensed is negotiation.

14. *To get things done and make things happen* you must bargain and trade rather than overpower and dominate. Leadership is usually coalition behavior rather than intimidation and punishment of enemies while rewarding friends. This moves negotiation into the key position among the managerial and professional techniques in our time.

15. *Most organizations have multiple objectives,* many of which are mutually exclusive. Making trade-offs between competing goals is a necessary skill of leadership, and trading off is the province of negotia-

tion. We could produce better-quality cars if we didn't have to make them economically, or meet customer demands. We could cut costs if we didn't worry about quality. We could achieve perfect efficiency if we didn't have to consider environmental impact and the health of workers at the same time as we achieve efficiency. Balancing these conflicting demands is done only by negotiation.

THE SEARCH FOR UNITY

Herman Hickman, long-time football coach at Yale, used to describe his relationship with the alumni as "keeping them sullen but not mutinous." This adroit phrase seems to many to be the temper of the times for leaders everywhere.

The ultimate purpose of negotiation is to seek—and probably never find—a condition which Mary Parker Follet called *unity*. This condition exists when all people find the world to be a place in which everyone's needs, desires, and interests are met more often than not. It doesn't mean that everyone will get everything they want, for this is impossible when two or more people have what seem to be mutually exclusive goals. Two men want to marry the same woman. Two competitors want to capture a majority of the market share. The purchasing agent wants lower prices, and the salesman wants the highest possible price. Unions seek high wages and benefits, while their employers seek lower labor costs per unit.

The age of negotiations produces another ideal or norm. The key to successful negotiations is the ability to redefine and shuffle self-interests—yours and the other party's—to attain a workable agreement. Life and commerce can then proceed. Each party will bring goals, needs, resources, and power to the negotiations, expecting to influence the other side, and also expecting to be influenced in return. The search for unity in the age of negotiations will produce some of the following consequences for managers and workers.

1. *The pressure to egalitarianism* will continue to mount, and satisfaction of the many will take the place of the privilege of the few. John Gardner as a young professor once described an inscription on a college blackboard as he entered the room to administer a final exam. Some wag—probably far ahead of his time—had scrawled on the board, "Every man an A student," and below it, "Share the grades!"[1] If this should smother the motivation to achieve excellence and quality, it will

be unnoticed if people get more of their own way. Unity means that more people will be satisfied, and the means by which this unity can be achieved is actually quite circumscribed: it can only be done when negotiation skills become widespread and common.

2. *Tough-minded management takes on a new meaning.* Being tough-minded doesn't mean being mean-spirited, brutal in action, or harsh in language. Rather it means having a high tolerance for frustration, a thick skin, a capacity to bounce back when you hit an obstacle. It means a willingness to stick with tough decisions in the face of strident minority pressure, patience to wait for things to run their course before making changes, and persistence in making changes by moving others who resist change.

For many, this age of negotiations will seem to be an impossible world. For many older executives the best outcome will seem to be to retreat to a retirement community where only people over sixty may reside, and the only people admitted under the age of thirty will be those driving liquor trucks.

For the future executive, however, this age of negotiations will be one of excitement, challenge, and exhilaration. As the German Chancellor Konrad Adenauer once put it, "A thick skin can be a gift from god."

2
Stemming Depersonalization Through Negotiations

"When a person's whole attention is bestowed on the seventeenth part of a pin, or the eightieth part of a button" he becomes stupid. Such was the conclusion of Adam Smith, the wise Scottish economist who wrote *Wealth of Nations* in 1776 and accordingly became known as the theoretical father of capitalism—or at least of an industrial society. Smith suggested that the division of labor into small parts would increase the wealth of nations, raise the standard of living, increase our health, and eliminate poverty. But he also noted some drawbacks, the main one being that this finely honed division of labor could reduce the worker in an industrial society to a mere instrument of the organization. "Further," he added, "commerce sinks courage."[1]

The truth of this dire prediction is still with us, and many clerks in insurance companies, sitting before a boob tube tapping inputs into a computer, or checking copies against originals, are assailed with the distinct impression that they are indeed not wholly functioning persons.

Yet this reduction of people to instruments of the industrial machine hasn't been without its countermovements. Since 1960 it has become apparent that people bring new expectations to their jobs which earlier workers in the industrial society didn't.

HOW BUREAUCRACY CREATES APATHY IN ITS OWN RANKS

The standards of living of people in an industrial society are fabulously better than in the Middle Ages. The division of labor, the accumulation of large sums of capital, and the full development of technology have benefited everyone to some degree, even the lowest-level worker. Few would like to return to the Middle Ages except perhaps a few sociopaths who join communes in Vermont or California. At the same time, for the population at large there are discontents in civilization, and the effects of these discontents show up in several ways.

We find that employees become apathetic when their work is routine, monotonous, and repetitive. There is within all of us, Fiske and Maadi propose, a desire for *varied experience,* which is all too often denied by the deadening routine of the bureaucratic organization,[2] whether in a corporation, government agency, school, or voluntary organization. This apathy can produce some rebellion in a variety of forms. Unionization is essentially a protest movement, sometimes over wages, but even when pay is generous, people rebel over work conditions that stifle individuality and self-expression.

A few years back, one of the authors conducted at company request an attitude survey of the employees of a large Eastern railroad. The study consisted of going from job to job and asking various workers what they liked best and least about their work. One category queried were skilled operators in a classification yard. One hot August afternoon we climbed into a tower overlooking a yard where freight cars were rolled over a hump by yard engines, at which time they were routed to assigned tracks to make up chains of cars for long hauls later that night. Standing in the tower alone, the controller would switch the cars onto the track assigned by a teletype. After being placed on the right track, the cars rolled down a decline to connect with other cars in that spur. In order to prevent their crashing too heavily into the cars already there, retarders on the tracks were operated in relays to brake the cars, the retarders clamping against the flanges of the cars, slowing them down to reasonable speeds. The glass-enclosed tower was equipped with a teletype, a board for switching cars to the right track, and a bank of retarders to slow the car as it rolled down on its track.

The day was hot and humid and the inside of the tower was ovenlike, causing the operator to sweat profusely. The attention demanded was intense and unremitting. Car after car rolled over the hump, requiring simultaneous action on the teletype, switcher, and retarder.

"What do you like best about your job?" the subject was asked.

"This is a high-paying job" was the reply.

"What are the major things you don't like about your work?" came next.

"It's hotter than hell up here," came the response. "It would be a lot cooler if the company would hang up a shade on the west window for hot afternoons like this," he added. "I've told 'em about it before."

"Do you have any other problems?"

"Oh, yes, on hot afternoons like this sometimes the retarders don't connect the way they should. Some day one of those flatcars of steel is going to break loose and tear up the whole yard. We'll have a derailment, cars spilling all over, and the whole yard will be tied up for several days until they straighten it out."

"Have you told the management about these defective retarders?" he was asked.

"Hell no. I told them about the shades. They can find out about the defective retarders themselves."

The point of this shop tale, which could be duplicated with different details again and again, is clear. People at work have many opportunities to advise management about things that would benefit the organization and the management, but they aren't inclined to do so when the things that affect them personally aren't heeded.

The widespread presence of malicious obedience is another form of silent rebellion against the depersonalizing nature of work in many organizations. The engineer whose work is divided into finer and finer minutiae without offering a picture of the entire task and objective, accompanied by the bosses' disregard of any statements of personal needs, wants, desires, and aspirations, produces anger and rebellion, which if ineffective settles soon into mere apathy. "Let 'em find out themselves" is a recourse an apathetic worker can adopt with impunity. The withheld suggestion, the idea never revealed, and the ability never used will remain invisible to the management except in an overall result of lost productivity, bad work, defective product, and lack of cooperation.

Extensive experience over the years asking workers, engineers, and middle managers their views of their work situation has produced again and again the bitter questions: "Does anybody up there know what I want to do, do they know what I can do, do they even know what I am doing?" These three questions are symptomatic of a worker malaise, which Opinion Research Corporations studies show have reached the highest levels ever during the early eighties, including a rising discontent among middle managers as well as workers.[3]

Herbert Marcuse, the intellectual guru of a generation of campus radicals during the sixties, wrote: "The distinguishing feature of advanced industrial society is its effective suffocation of those needs which demand liberation—liberation also from that which is tolerable and rewarding and comfortable, while it sustains and absolves the destructive power and repressive function of the affluent society."[4]

Many would argue that the repression is negligible compared with feudal societies which came before, or the repression in underdeveloped nations today. It did strike a strong emotional chord with many who could see that after all their education they could be reduced to robotic functions at work by the style of management then in use.

Apathy at work is a chronic concern of industrial societies, and leads to some of the following tangible effects:

1. *People withhold their best efforts* when their opinions, interests, and needs aren't sought out and incorporated into the way things are done.

2. *This apathy produces declining levels of productivity* for people who do merely that which is put before them. Legions of workers are withholding ideas, problem solutions, and innovations which could make things better, cheaper, safer, faster, and more economical at work. The loss of commitment to the purposes of the organization is a tangible loss which shows in the bottom line of product, markets, and profits.

3. *Quality suffers when employees are apathetic.* The mistake which could have been prevented by alert and committed people isn't prevented, and nobody cares. The mixed-up wiring, the missing weld, the press which produces scrap are all end results of worker apathy.

4. *Passive and dependent people at work* become passive and dependent citizens. The chances of a nation resisting overpowering government, or manipulation by a demagogue, is lessened when the bulk of their citizens' working hours are spent doing dull things not of their own choosing, and in which they cannot participate. Participative management in the past has all too often been fallaciously identified with some kind of sentimental democracy in which bosses poll their employees, or take votes on decisions. This model is of course not only impractical in most organizations, but even if implemented would do nothing more than slow up the works without satisfying the employees. Participation through negotiation, however, is a more personal process, matching the needs of the individual with the needs of the organization.

THE CUSTOMER'S WAR AGAINST BUREAUCRACY

A few years ago a group of students in a large business school undertook an investigation of how corporations process customer complaints. They found that one firm had a WATS line, with a free 800 number which a disgruntled customer could call. This was intended to provide a listening ear for unhappy consumers whose satisfaction with the company's product was less than ecstatic.

The first time the students placed a call to the number they were greeted by a tape-recorded message which went somewhat as follows: "All of the customer complaints lines are busy. Your call will be processed in the order in which it was received. Please wait. If you prefer, you may wait until the sound of the beep and leave a message which will be dealt with by our consumer relations staff at the first opportunity. Please leave your name and phone number."

Shocked at such an impersonal response to a grievance by a customer, the students conferred and devised a suitable response. They attached a tape recorder with a continual loop and their own phone with the following message being talked steadily into the company's tape recorder: "This is an angry customer. . . . Go to hell. This is an angry customer. . . . Go to hell," and so on ad infinitum.

However unusual this tape-recorded mechanism might be among customer relations departments, it is all too typical of how companies are responding to the rebellion of angry customers and clients. It completely misses the root of the problem of customer dissatisfaction. The problem isn't the immediate issue of a lemon, a dud, or a breakdown. It is the sense of powerlessness that buyers have learned to feel when they try to deal with a bureaucratic organization.

Rodney Cron, an expert in consumer service programs, points out that with the rapid rise in complaints by customers, consumer advocates are increasing and consumer groups are developing and expanding.[5] The causes lie deeper, he proposes, than in the quality of the goods and more in the rising level of expectations of the customers. Much of the surface expression of unhappiness may center upon the quality of the product, but the root cause is the failure of the manufacturer to really communicate with its customers. He proposes a two-stage process: *recognition* of the needs of the customer, and *demonstration* of a continuing positive responsiveness.

The rising level of consumerism is the end result of the sense of powerlessness that people feel when confronting the bureaucracy. Consumers have certain interests which they have converted into "rights." The rights include the right to be informed about the real nature of the product, the right to be safe in using products, the right to choose among alternatives based upon complete information, and the right to be heard. When these rights are missing, the consumer is apt to take recourse in pressure tactics, including legislative controls over corporations, as well as other rebellious actions, some of which may become downright unreasonable.

HOW BUREAUCRACY PRODUCES ALIENATED PEOPLE

When people work in a world in which they feel powerless, the vast majority will settle for their paycheck and let their outside interests provide their pleasures. They buy elegant campers, TV sets that show home movies and play games, and they take romantic vacations in exotic places. Work becomes more and more separated from their self-expression, which is to say from their real lives. "Apathy here, fun there" is a model of adaptation for millions of employed people, "Thank God it's Friday" a national philosophy.

Work thus becomes a pain to be endured as the price of having a sound income to enjoy the rewards of off-the-job living. The T-account of balancing entries of pleasure and pain is a perfectly satisfactory bargain for most; such is the accounting for life in affluent societies. Yet our prime time is spent at work; work makes the dominant demands on our energy and leaves our nonworking hours as incidental. To keep the books in balance means avoiding heavy commitments on the job which would detract from the physical and psychic energy needed for the life of enjoyment outside the workplace. People seek a life style first, then a job to support it. Few people will keep up a protracted revolution against a job that seems to be a time period devoid of intellectual and psychological satisfaction. They accept.

Yet there are some people, generally young and still unbroken by the need to submit, who rebel against the system in a variety of ways. These are the alienated. For a time during the sixties they drew an unprecedented amount of public attention—publicity at least—in the campus revolts of the period. Most have long since abandoned such juvenile pastimes. Radical student leaders now engage in such occupations as securities analyst, government administrator, or some kind of self-employment at meager craft occupations. They often hang onto the key elements of their earlier discontent, and thus assure that they won't really get ahead in the traditional "success" game.

Alienated people in our society, however small their numbers, are nonetheless important, for they produce effects which are hardly beneficial. Here is how alienated people impact an industrial society.

1. *They attack the basis of the society, not its details.* The radical student, economist, or citizen isn't concerned about the specifics of unfairness, injustice, or inequalities, but the system which produced them. Thus, the whole establishment which enjoys the successes within the system is considered wrong. What radicals call for is not reform but revolution. They may attack the school system as an agent of the system which they despise, the goal being not educational reform but a total upset of the entire system.

2. *They are often the most perceptive and intelligent people.* It was not at Podunk Teacher's or some backwater college that the radicalism of the sixties flourished, but at Berkeley, Michigan, Columbia, and similar elite educational institutions. The students there were screened for admission on the basis of intelligence and promise, for the most part. Yet it was in these academies of the elite that the alienation seemed highest.

3. *When they don't win their wars they retreat from society.* The more militant of the alienated often tried to break down society by battling against it, sometimes physically. Such a revolution was of course doomed from the start. Having neither the maturity, the discipline, the means of financing a war, nor public support, the radicals ended up with broken heads and disillusionment about the possibility of winning their war. The next-best alternative seemed to be to flee the entire scene and join a commune or counterculture society, or adopt some individual strategy of retreating from the balance-sheet world which requires work that offers them little self-expression. Drugs, religious cults, and endless varieties of gurus flourished.

4. *The questions radicals ask are far better than their answers.* If there is a contribution to be found in the revolt of the alienated, it lies in the questions they ask: Why should we be so deeply enmeshed in arms production in the world when people are starving? How can we care for the old who can no longer take care of themselves? Why should people be pressed into doing things they know are absurd in order to make a living? These are all fine questions that every citizen, conservative or otherwise, should have on his agenda if he would preserve the best features of our society.

It was their answers which were trivial, ineffective, or even worse; boring as all get out. Nothing impressed me more from my observations of the campus radicals of the sixties than the utter banality of their suggested antidotes. They repeated incantations of a crushingly boring Marxist dialectic, or infantile prescriptions that any freshman in economics could see through.

One student at Hampshire College informed me with passion that the multinationals should be disbanded because "they produce bread which has sawdust in it." It's undoubtedly important to study carefully the impact of the growing multinational corporations (MNC) upon international relations and the possibilities of international peace. As a human innovation, the MNC has made its mark and will do so even more in the future. What direction should it take and how should it be governed? These are good questions. The answers of the alienated, however, are for the most part irrelevant and in many small ways rubbish.

WAYS NEGOTIATIONS EASE DEPERSONALIZATION

Negotiation has numerous qualities which can be brought to bear upon the dilemmas we've cited in this chapter. Here are some of the ways in which negotiation has emerged in such a role.

1. *Negotiation is a vehicle of commercial trade.* In commercial trade, negotiating means transferring something of value to another in return for something of equal value. This is what the purchasing agent and salesperson do. Negotiation is the foundation of the marketplace, and the culture surrounding such dealing is as old as history. People bring things of value to a place where they can barter, offering things of which they have a surplus and which others do not have. The other party brings a similar package of goodies to the market, and they haggle and bargain face-to-face with offers and counteroffers until a deal is struck and the exchange completed.

2. *Negotiation means to confer with another face-to-face.* Embedded in the very essence of negotiation is the crucial requirement that bargaining, conflict resolution, and changing another's opinion must occur in face-to-face contact, with verbal and bodily communication occurring simultaneously by both parties. You can't produce real negotiation by written means. Only confirmations of bargains can be handled by written instruments. The final product of a bargain is most likely a written agreement or contract. The contract is not the negotiation, but its tangible end result. The discussion in negotiations is the substance of

the process. The other person should be listened to, responded to, and acted upon. It is a noncoercive, persuasive, and hortatory process.

3. *Negotiation means to deal with, manage, or conduct*. The Japanese fleet, it is said, "negotiated the straits of Suragao" at night to engage the American fleet at the battle of Leyte Gulf. President Carter negotiated between the national shoals of Egyptian and Israeli interests to produce a new Near East policy at Camp David. Shoals and rocks lay on every side, but they were "negotiated."

4. *It means clearing hurdles and overcoming obstacles*. The Third Army of General George S. Patton had to "negotiate" the hedgerows of Normandy before it could spring free for its sweeping runs across the plains of France to the German border. The manager or business person must negotiate legal, social, and cultural barriers to build a new shopping center or high-rise apartment, or to create a merger with a competing firm. The hedgerows may be arboreal, legal, social, cultural, or emotional. The negotiation process isn't simply knocking over the hurdles and barriers, but occasionally going over them, around them, and under them as well as through them; no fixed pattern is possible to prescribe for any individual situation.

5. *It means knowing your goals with crystal clarity*. Negotiation is the means of attaining what to you is an important purpose, aim, mission, or objective. If you don't know where you are headed, any outcome will be satisfactory. If you aim for nothing, that is about what you will hit. Your expectations defined in advance will be the guide for action in negotiation.

6. *Negotiation is impossible without adaptation*. The ability to change when confronted with obstacles and barriers, and to avoid fixed behavior and rigidity, are the qualities that people need most in negotiations. Jean Baptiste Lamarck, an early pioneer in biology, suggested that evolution and progress follow four elements: being goals-centered, being adaptive, making major changes when needed, and having memories of the past. Negotiation is in large part a matter of adaptation in order to keep moving toward established goals.

7. *Negotiation is a major strategy, not a simple package of behaviors*. The ancient Phoenecians expanded their empire by concentrating on possession of seacoastal areas in order to carry on their trade. General Douglas MacArthur in World War II skipped from island to island, capturing and holding only perimeter enclaves as he "negotiated" his

way back to the Philippines and beyond. Negotiation thus consists of giving up some major elements of your possible desires in order to win those which are absolutely essential to your goals.

8. *Negotiation means arranging things in order to win what is important to you.* Negotiation often calls for manipulation of several variables. The triangle trade of buying in one market to sell in another in order to acquire the means of getting a third product you truly desire is an example of such an arrangement. President Reagan thus could trade wheat to the Russians in 1981 at the same time that he denied them other ameneties or even civilities because they had invaded Afghanistan. He could thus shore up his political strength with his farm constituencies in order to gain the power to win key battles in Congress, and perhaps control over his own policies and objectives.

NEGOTIATION HEIGHTENS THE IMPORTANCE OF THE NEGOTIATOR

From these varied aspects of negotiations some conclusions emerge which suggest that negotiation meets many of the requirements of self-actualization of people in a depersonalized world. Here are the ways in which negotiation—and systematic use of negotiation—personalize and enliven an otherwise depersonalized life for the negotiators.

1. *Negotiation is never the same from case to case.* The convoluted history of Ambassador Habib's negotiations in 1981 as he skipped from Israel to Saudi Arabia to Lebanon in an attempt to defuse a latent war between the Israeli and the PLO would require volumes of written transcript to describe. The processes by which a labor contract is finally settled, or a commercial contract concluded, or a set of objectives for a general manager written, a divorce settlement resolved are never identical, Each calls forth the intense personal effort of the parties, and never is the process the same from example to example.

2. *There are some common patterns of negotiation which can be helpful.* Like the clinical case book of the psychiatrist, negotiations, despite their diversity, have overall patterns of regularity which are useful to study and practice. There are patterns for dealing with Arabs, Japanese, or Latin Americans which can be studied and applied by negotiators with each of these groups. As in war, where an unexpected thunderstorm, or the burning of a filament in a computer, can decide the

issue, individual small variations are often crucial. Nonetheless, learning the patterns of negotiation can assure that you won't fall into big traps due to inexperience.

3. *The personality and behavior of the negotiator are important.* Face-to-face communication results in an exchange of meaning, and the entire personality of the negotiator is involved. Ultimately, negotiation is a test of the self. Nothing could be more personalized than negotiation, despite its adherence to certain overall patterns of strategy and tactics which experienced negotiators have mastered.

4. *Both sides can win in negotiation.* The difference between negotiation and combat or domination is that both sides can win in negotiation. If a subordinate has expressed his interests, needs, desires, and talents in the negotiations process, that in itself may be a victory, if such self-expression was the objective to begin with. The symbolic terms of "victory" and "defeat" are often not the true objective, more important are the achievement of personal goals, the saving of face, the retention of respect, and the development of self-esteem. "Unconditional surrender" is a term of victory and defeat, and domination. "Lock the union out for Christmas" is an expression of war. Negotiating in the newspapers, as occurred in the baseball strike of 1981, was aimed at domination rather than agreement and unity. As a result, both sides lost heavily. The win-lose mind-set is not present in sound negotiations; a win-win objective is the aim.

In this book, the major emphasis is upon the overall patterns of strategy which characterize successful negotiation. To the extent possible, we'll illustrate the informal, chaotic, and sometimes bizarre nature of the process as well.

Check your own practices against these fourteen guides to develop a stronger negotiating strategy:

	Never	Sometimes	Always
1. Do you expect to gain something and also to lose something?	—	—	—
2. Will you bend in values as well as in tangible things?	—	—	—
3. Do you seek mutual agreement rather than giving orders?	—	—	—

	Never	Sometimes	Always
4. Do you avoid being hung up on your customary values in special situations?	—	—	—
5. Do you negotiate for the long haul as well as for immediate issues?	—	—	—
6. Do you find common areas of interest as well as the diverse ones?	—	—	—
7. Can you easily see areas of interdependence with the other side?	—	—	—
8. Do you keep third parties out of your negotiations?	—	—	—
9. Do you avoid trying to apply firm rules and procedures to negotiating?	—	—	—
10. Do you genuinely recognize the ways in which you need the other party?	—	—	—
11. Do you always seek to induce responses from the other side?	—	—	—
12. Do you avoid overcomplicating the issues in negotiation and seek simplicity?	—	—	—
13. Do you consider third parties' interests in negotiations?	—	—	—
14. Can you avoid zero-sum thinking in negotiations?	—	—	—

Give yourself one point for every "Sometimes," two points for every "Never." A score of 0–5 is excellent; 6–10 fair; over 10 poor.

3
Developing and Using a Personal Strategy for Negotiation

> "Your face, my Thane, is as a book
> where men may read strange matters."
> —*Macbeth*

The mother of one of the authors, a genteel lady of New England ancestry, was a special kind of negotiator. Her strategy for getting other people to do things she would like to have them do was to appear helpless. One day in the 1930s she returned from Boston on the train and sought a taxi at the Lowell station. The train was packed with businessmen, rushing agressively about and pushing others out of the way to get the few available cabs. Mother, dragging a tired and grouchy infant son behind her, got *three* of them. She simply walked out into the middle of the street in the rain, water pouring off her fancy hat, and stood there, helpless. Not one, but three cab drivers rushed out to whisk her into their cab. "For gosh sakes, lady, you and that child will catch your death of cold standing out there, get in." All of the businessmen stepped aside as she triumphantly swept into the one of her choice and drove away. She made her helplessness her major strategy of negotiation. Helpless? Like General Motors or the U.S. Marine Corps. She knew exactly what she was doing and played up her apparent naiveté and dependency to get everyone on her side.

Jimmy Hoffa, on the other hand, was dependent upon nobody. "Life is a jungle," he told a television interviewer. He played his role to the hilt. Tough, aggressive, he threatened, ranted, swindled, bribed, and beat up those who got in his path. His reputation for bargaining was that he bargained iron tough. He instilled fear in many he dealt with, and they backed off, bowed, and deferred lest they draw the fire of his drive to fight and win by whatever means. He ultimately disappeared one day amidst speculation that he had been done in by the mob, and mystery still surrounds this aggressive, mean, colorful, and wholly intractable little man. He bribed jurors, diverted large sums from union funds for his personal use, and bought people he couldn't whip. Coupled with boundless energy, his toughness comprised a negotiating strategy which won his union members generous salaries and lucrative contracts, for which they rewarded him again and again by reelecting him president of the Teamsters.

The point, of course, isn't that my mother could have acted like Jimmy Hoffa, for she was constitutionally unable to dominate anyone by force, all the while getting her way easily. Nor could Jimmy Hoffa look anything but the fool if he had tried upon his adversaries her strategy of vulnerability and dependence. It might even have been a momentary act of trusting the mobsters for a private meeting that led to his downfall. The point here is that you should have a personal negotiation strategy which suits you, and which you have fine-tuned through successive experiments.

FIFTEEN BUILDING BLOCKS OF A PERSONAL STRATEGY FOR NEGOTIATION

How should you choose a general strategic pattern for your negotiations, whether it be in collective bargaining, in commercial transactions, or in dealing with bosses and subordinates? There are fifteen areas in which you must answer questions for your own clarification. The end result is that you can craft a strategy for transacting that will work best for you, in the situations you ordinarily encounter.

RULE 1. Expect to gain something, expect to lose something.

In professional baseball, the negotiation of player contracts is strongly shaped by an arbitration clause which was negotiated into the agreement between clubs and players. Each year the individual players negotiate with owners for salary rates. The player makes one demand, the owner makes another offer. If they can't find some middle number in between, the disagreement is then, according to the negotiated contract between the parties, submitted to the arbitration process. A neutral third party hears the arguments of both sides. Unlike ordinary labor arbitration, however, in which the arbitrator may choose either position or some position in between, only one option is open to the arbitrator according to the terms of the negotiated contract.

He must choose either the player's request or the owner's offer.

Thus if Reggie Jackson asks $2.1 million and the club offers $1.5 million, the arbitrator must choose either Reggie's demand or the owner's offer: No middle ground is allowed. This has several effects. It makes it imperative that the individual bargainers arrive at some kind of middle ground or they face the chance of losing heavily at the hands of the third party. For another thing, it causes people to move voluntarily during the negotiations. All parties realize that they have something to win and something to lose.

In every negotiation you should be prepared to bend. Demanding unconditional surrender is a bad strategy. You can't be stiff-necked, arbitrary, sanctimoniously right, or rigid in negotiating with others.

RULE 2. You have to bend in values as well as in tangible goods.

Having a passion for some worthy cause, being a crusader or a missionary for a noble cause, may put you in a special class of humanity. It also makes you a rotten negotiator if it impels you to be unbending. The True Believer is a fanatic, and has kept wars, feuds, and impasses going for longer than was necessary. The achievement of peace and progress which accompanies it is important to getting where you want to go, and using the negotiation table as a place to impose your values whole on the other side could prevent you from making progress in your desired aims. This doesn't mean you give up your values, but rather that you allow the other person to have theirs as well.

In one Midwestern utility a somewhat puritanical manager was determined not to allow any kickbacks or slippery arrangements to upset the bidding process for contracted work. When final negotiations seemed to be near, one of the contractors sought a mild bribe. "I'd like a $6,000 country club membership for myself worked into the arrangement," he proposed. "Other managers have done this in the past," he explained. Offended by this flagrant attempt at personal extortion, the straight-laced manager resolved the problem with a counteroffer. "Sure, Bill, I'll write it right into the contract and we'll both sign it," he responded. The other, faced with what would be an obvious revelation of his grafting scheme, quickly backed off.

RULE 3. Mutual agreements are not achieved by directives and orders.

When the other party has the power to withhold something or to punish, you are hardly in a position to direct them as if they were subordinates or lackeys. You must deal.

Many years ago in India one of the authors owned an old watch which finally quit operating. Taking it to a local repairperson, he left it for an estimate. When he returned to get the estimate, he was shown his watch completely disassembled, the parts strewn on a rag. The repairperson named a high price for repairing it. Viewing the innards of his watch displayed before him, the customer knew he had diminished his role as boss and customer. His options at this point were constrained by the situation. He could order the wily repairperson to reassemble the watch and take it to another shop. Unfortunately this probably would have meant that the watch would never run again, for some vital part might be lost, or gears reversed in assembly. Sadly he realized that he was no longer boss and began a weak effort to negotiate a best possible price, which turned out to be more than the watch was worth.

RULE 4. Customary values may be meaningless in negotiation.

In picking a strategy for an upcoming deal, you may have in mind a clear figure as to the worth of what the other person is selling or offering. Such values, however, are merely a starting place for negotiations and may or may not relate to what will finally be paid.

Take the case of the isolated store, with no other supplier around for miles. You need an item very badly. You find an all-night store open, and they ask five dollars for a razor. You have no razor and badly need a shave the next morning for an important meeting. The best bet is to forget the fact that your local druggist would sell you the item for sixty cents. Start negotiating from the five dollar price downward, and any reduction you can get off that asking price should be considered a victory.

RULE 5. Negotiate for the long haul as well as the immediate issue.

Sometimes a clever victory in negotiations when you have the other person over a barrel will cost you more in the long run than some bending to their blandishments and persuasion. The purchasing agent who squeezes a good supplier to the point of no profit or a sizable loss may find that they will reluctantly go elsewhere with their wares in the future. The idea is to maximize advantage over the foreseeable future, not to exact immediate winnings. Negotiate to win, allowing the other side to win too. The objective is to capture, not destroy. The new claims manager in a large insurance firm sought to establish his profit-making abilities too strongly. He saved the company thousands of dollars in claims—and lost substantial business for the sales force in the process. The big customer, the important client, and the steady provider should be treated differently than the one-time peddler. If you have to live with somebody for years ahead, it's sensible to let them win something to build the relationship to the mutual advantage of both.

RULE 6. The objectives of the parties are both common and diverse.

Finding coalition and unity calls for recognizing when you have things in common, and when you differ. If you are the boss setting objectives for a subordinate, it's true that the subordinate needs the job badly in many cases, which gives you some clout in setting goals. But if you set those goals impossibly high you are building failure into the relationship and perhaps destroying the relationship. You get a bad employee which you yourself created. The company needs good employees as much as the employee needs the job and a paycheck. They thus have a common interest in settling tough and attainable goals which will stretch the employee, at the same time as they permit him to succeed and prosper.

RULE 7. In negotiation the parties are interdependent.

In a large auto parts factory an important machine broke down and an expert was called in to repair it. Time was costing the company money. Under the stern and critical eye of the plant manager, the serviceperson from the manufacturer surveyed the mess, and then calmly proceeded to open his lunch bucket and thermos jug. The plant manager started a tirade, demanding that he drop lunch and start fixing the machine. "The line is down, it's costing me thousands of dollars every day this thing is down. So get to work!" The serviceperson quietly thought about the demand: "Buddy, if you want to be helpful, why don't you get me some sugar for my coffee. My wife didn't put any in this morning when

I left home. Remember, pal, you need me as much as I need you." The manager fumed a couple of minutes, then sent a nearby worker to the cafeteria for some sugar.

It's important to size up who needs whom before you start making demands. Often negotiation reverses traditional authority relationship, for the parties need each other at different levels.

RULE 8. A decision made between the parties is better than one imposed by outsiders.

In the heat of bargaining, one side or the other may act hastily in such a fashion that it forces the dispute into the courts, arbitration, or the press, or moves the problem to a higher-level executive office. Usually such third-party solutions are risky. Good labor negotiators usually know that it is unwise to arbitrate *interests* such as the size of a pay raise, or the cost of benefits. It is far better to settle the issue between the two parties, however long and exhausting the process of settlement may be, for each can thus hang onto those small but important gains which sweeten the settlement for both sides.

Parties to negotiating have stronger motives than third parties. A water utility in the West needed a coffer dam to divert a stream and contracted with a local contractor to build it for $200,000. It was to be completed in thirty days, and removed five months later. Half the fee, $100,000 was to be paid upon completion, and the other half upon removal. The dam was completed on schedule and the first payment delivered. Then, due to factors beyond the control of either party, it was concluded that the dam should remain in place for another six months. The contractor sought to renegotiate the price for removal to allow for the delay. The utility insisted that it owed nothing more. How would you approach this case? From the viewpoint of the contractor, there was a cash outlay which would be tied up for another year; the cost of construction for the first half was actually higher than the fee paid; and the profit would come only at the end of the job. The utility had no choice but to insist that the dam be kept in place—and not removed—for another half year. How would you approach this from the viewpoint of the utility? Of the contractor?

As contractor, you might sue for a higher fee, you might try commercial arbitration, or you might appeal over the head of management to their board of directors. You might go to the press with your story.

Any of these three might win you more money, or partial payments. They might also cost you future business, lead to more exacting demands in performance, and thus add to your costs. The obvious strategy here was to negotiate one-on-one without interjecting third parties.

RULE 9. There are fewer rules in negotiation than we might like.

Invoking law or custom as a club in negotiations is usually worthless if not harmful. The rules of evidence, practice, and precedent may have to be set aside in hard negotiations, and the rules are those set by the participants in view of the particular situation.

Take the case of the office manager who was assigned a new group of employees, one of whom was an attractive lady. Her skills weren't up to the manager's standards and he decided to fire her, but was under instructions to check all major personnel actions with Mr. X, the higher-up boss. After several unsuccessful attempts to open the subject with the boss in the hectic office environment, the manager decided to go to Mr. X's home on Sunday morning to resolve the issue. He rang the bell and the door was answered by the offending attractive lady clad in a dressing gown. The manager immediately decided that the customary rules of organization would probably have to be suspended in this case.

RULE 10. An adjusted decision is better than no decision.

It is perfectly sound technique to enter the negotiations with some firm ideas of what you need, want, and must have. But as the situation evolves, your definitions of needs, wants, and must-haves should be flexible in response to the evolving bargaining.

A large brewery faced with heavy competition from large national competitors was losing sales each year. A new sales manager was hired, based upon his past record of spectacular success. It was agreed that if anybody could do the job, he could, and if he failed, nobody could do it. When the time came to set sales goals for the year, the management demanded an average upturn of ten percent per month. The new sales manager shrugged his shoulders and stated flatly that five percent was the maximum he would promise, and he insisted that that goal be firmed up in writing in advance. After a brief caucus in the hall, the management concluded that a five-percent gain was better than a continued decline, and signed the agreement.

Recognize your need for the other party. When you start negotiating with the mental set that the other party is wholly useless and can't really offer you a thing, you doom the whole process to failure. It's more sensible and more conducive to a good bargain to privately make a list of the things the other person has that you *want*, the things they have that you *need*, and the things you *must have*.

A large publisher became disenchanted with one of his editors and made up his mind to fire her. Under our urgings, he was asked to prepare such a list. "The only thing I *want* from her is her absence from my premises, I *need* that, and I guess I *must have it*." He smiled smugly. We probed him about her performance and behavior on the job over the past couple of years. It seemed that she did have strong personal ties to a couple of good authors who the company badly wanted to keep, and if she took those authors with her it would be a serious loss. Under some intense questioning, he recalled that one day she had slipped on a rug and broken a bone in her ankle which had never completely healed. "That's another thing, she is always playing for sympathy, using a little twinge of pain to take time off, which is very upsetting to the office." After further inquiry, it was divulged that she had never pressed the company for workmen's compensation claims beyond what was voluntarily offered. We asked a hypothetical question: Suppose she leaves under circumstances that make her furious and goes to a lawyer about her injury? Do you suppose she might win a suit? "Add that to my list of things I *want very much* not to happen. Thank you for pointing out this possibility." The separation was both generous and genial, and was sweetened by a year-long consulting editorship for the once "useless" employee. This outcome did not occur because she demanded it, but because she had the potential to do so, and the publisher came to recognize it.

RULE 11. Negotiation requires inducing a response from the other party.

An auto salesman of our acquaintance has a technique for dealing with potential customers which he explained thus. "I always make every effort for TSC in talking to a customer. That means *total situation control*. I do that by a long-rehearsed and well-polished sales pitch. I anticipate every question, rebut every possible argument, and try to jam them into the car and get them to sign before they can open their mouth." His boss told us: "Bill is not one of our best salesmen. He tries too hard and never lets the customer get a word in edgewise. He is the old-fashioned kind of used-car salesman that has given us a bad image, and furthermore it doesn't move cars because he never lets them talk themselves into a sale."

Talking a blue streak at the other side will keep them from bringing up their arguments, threats, promises, and offers to deal, and therefore these things can't be dealt with.

You don't have to *like* what the other person has to say, and in fact you may be infuriated or turned off by them, but unless you act in a way that gets the other person's demands out on the table, there is no hope of lasting agreement. An antiques dealer learned of an old chair owned by an elderly lady and decided to try to buy it. Using every ounce of charm and persuasion, he descended upon what was expected to be a hapless victim. His spiel began with an offhand statement about his considering buying the object, which he then derided scornfully to run down its value. He never let her get in a word edgewise, and he concluded: "Of course I couldn't offer you a cent more than $500 for it." The nice old lady accepted it meekly. Later she told us: "I really would have asked only $100 for it, but he never let me tell him what I was asking, he was so busy with his own presentation." The dealer never knew he had talked himself out of $400 by his failure to induce a response.

RULE 12. Keep negotiations as simple as you can.

Remember that negotiation at its simplest is conducting a discussion to reach agreement through exchange of information, appeals, a discussion of advantages and disadvantages, and conditional statements such as "If you will do thus, I will do so." Often in collective bargaining, purchasing, or other areas, the bargainers have a tendency to take a simple deal and complicate it into the merger of four Eastern railroads in bankruptcy conducted by twenty Philadelphia lawyers. It is possible to outsmart yourself by complicating the obvious.

In one Midwestern firm young Merrill had been hired from a consulting psychologist's staff. During the negotiations, Merrill had expressed a desire to get out of psychological interviewing and into labor relations. The company's personnel manager, however, wanted him to clean up a large backlog of needed psychological interviews with company personnel. Merrill agreed that he would join the company and clean up the backlog, after which he would be offered a chance to move over into labor relations. All went well until six months were up and the interviews completed. The personnel manager then went into agonies of convoluted thinking. Perhaps he would like to remain in the assessment department; maybe he would prefer to get plant experience in employment, or maybe a stretch in salary administration duties. As he arrayed the options, he quietyly picked up the phone and called Merrill. "Hey, Merrill, you have finished the interviews, I understand. Are you still interested in moving into the collective bargaining group?" The reply was prompt and emphatic. "You bet, when do I start?" The negotiations were simple, direct, and complete. The personnel manager stood on the brink of messing up a simple deal by overcomplicating it.

RULE 13. Always remember any third-party interest when dealing.

In 1981 when the Congress and President Ronald Reagan were at loggerheads over whether the United States should sell the complex AWACS plane to the Saudis, the principle of third-party interest was paramount. If they sold the planes to the Saudis it would help erect a protective shield of surveillance against Russian intervention into the oil-rich Middle East. At the same time, the planes had the potential of being used in any Saudi forays against our longtime ally Israel. The Israelis' friends worked diligently to quash the whole deal. It left the Administration with a negotiating straddle between two powers with whom it was friendly, but who didn't get along with each other in any way.

A large milk company was in collective bargaining with the union for drivers and inside workers at the creamery. The union pressed strongly, with a solid strike vote of their members backing their demands. Under this pressure, the company conceded to their demands. Later when they attempted to raise the price of milk to cover the costs of the raise which had been negotiated amidst friendly handshakes between management and labor, they were rejected flatly by the state milk control board. The company had completely forgotten the third party who was a shadow negotiator at the sessions. The negotiations had the surface appearance of being one-to-one, but the third party was nonetheless there, and in the end the company lost heavily in profits because it hadn't reviewed the third-party interests in the case.

RULE 14. The material objects and money involved often aren't the most important ingredients in negotiations but are symbolic.

Take the case of Jerry, a highly talented expert in computer design. He received an attractive offer from another firm and notified his boss of the offer and hinted strongly that he was probably going to take it. The boss immediately responded by promising to meet every competitive offer, penny for penny. Jerry wavered but still seemed ready to move out. At the suggestion of a personnel manager, the boss then asked Jerry, "Are there any other conditions in your work which we could change to make it attractive for you to stay?" Jerry was hesitant for a minute and then stated, "Sure, I would stay if I could get an office with a window. I have worked here five years in an inside office without a window. As you know I am a hiker, fisherman, and jogger and love the outdoors. It has been a constant thorn in my side that I haven't been able to see trees and grass from my workplace, and I would like to be moved." Astonished at such a minor demand taking such heightened importance, the boss quickly agreed, and even offered Jerry a corner office with glass on two sides and a view of a brook. Jerry quickly accepted and called the other firm to reject the outside job offer.

The development of understanding, belief, trust, acceptance, and respect through exchange, new combinations, and collaboration are just as important in negotiations as money. Through such methods both parties can win.

RULE 15. Avoid "zero-sum thinking" in planning your negotiations.

In mathematical decision making there is a concept called "zero sum" relationships. This means that everything I gain must necessarily mean a corresponding decline in your holdings. While this may be true in poker, where the whole payroll is on the table, it isn't true in the great majority of negotiating situations. Avoid getting caught in zero-sum thinking, but rather think about how both parties can win. As Robert Fisher of Harvard Law School describes traditional international negotiations, we have adhered to such zero-sum bargaining with the Russians. Past bargaining, he says, was comprised of three elements: (1)

Decide in advance exactly what your position is before talking to the other side. (2) Argue about positions by defending yours and attacking theirs. (3) Make every concession slowly, and then only to keep the talks from breaking down. But the avoidance of zero-sum talks is far superior as a negotiating technique. This might be labeled win-win negotiation. It too has three elements: (1) Talk about both parties' *interests* thoroughly before doing anything else. You should learn as much as possible about the other side's needs, wants, and interests before proposing anything. (2) Generate a lot of *options*. The more options you can propose, the more likely you will produce a quality decision which has high acceptance by both sides. (3) *Decide later*. With a grasp of the other person's interests and a lot of options available, some reciprocity can emerge. The negotiations might produce recommendations for official decisions later.

HOW TO USE THIS CHAPTER

Go over each of the fifteen rules and rate yourself on your strategic approach to negotiations. Where are your strengths and weaknesses? Do the techniques suggested fit your style, and if they don't, can you learn to use them? It will improve your negotiating results considerably.

4
Negotiation by Objectives

> If you don't know where you
> are going, then any road will
> get you there.
> —THE KORAN

In an Eastern telephone company a group of younger women formed a caucus to open new opportunities for women in nontraditional jobs, that is, jobs ordinarily held by men only. One such job entailed outdoor work, climbing poles and ladders, and doing skilled work. At their first appeal the women were rejected, supposedly not because of discrimination against their sex, but because, as the superintendent stated, "This job you are asking for requires that you carry around a seventy-pound ladder, and we don't think that's legal for women. Besides, how can a little 110-pound gal carry a seventy-pound ladder, lift it up and take it down? You'd hurt yourselves, so I guess the answer is no."

Undaunted by this argument, the women caucused and returned with a counterproposal. "Buy some aluminum ladders and they won't weigh seventy pounds but forty pounds and we can handle that." The male side caucused and returned with the information that aluminum might be unsafe because it was highly conductive of electricity and that on occasion they were required to work near power lines, and it would be too dangerous. The women caucused once more, and after some hasty phone calls suggested fiberglass ladders which would weigh thirty-eight pounds and be free of conductivity. The other side caucused and agreed. As one of them noted after the agreement was struck, "They'll be easier on the men too!"

In negotiations in this case each side got what it wanted, but neither achieved it in the way they had originally proposed. The men in the case had some specific goals. While they weren't opposed to women simply because of their sex, they were concerned about the reaction of crews if some of the males had to add chivalry to their job description and carry and raise ladders for the women on their crew as well as for themselves. The women wanted better-paying jobs, line experience, a chance to demonstrate their flexibility in job assignment, and thus more opportunity. Both gained from the negotiations without either side achieving exactly what they had started to obtain. Even though the fiberglass ladders were more expensive, the company obtained them, where they had resisted doing so earlier when the all-male crew had requested them. The best appeal is thus one which influences people by meeting *their* wants and needs, rather than simply hammering away about your own.

MAKING MBO WORK IN NEGOTIATIONS

The system of management known as Management by Objectives, MBO, is a commonly used method where bosses and subordinates sit down and jointly define the purposes, responsibilities, and major results sought in the subordinates' jobs. To make this work well requires that each party first meet privately and map out their ideas of what the job objectives should be. Then the two set a mutually convenient time and place and talk out the common areas of agreement about job objectives, and then proceed to defining the areas where agreement does not exist. Of course the boss has some firm requirements for the job, and it would be unrealistic to assume that the boss must always concede. Yet the process of negotiations is one in which each side states his or her concept of the job content, and the differences are ironed out.

Such a discussion should center upon results sought and the standards of performance for each job. At the end of the discussion the subordinate and boss should be in agreement on answers to two key questions: What is the job, and how will results be measured? Such a system works perfectly well in negotiations between people who are in something other than boss-subordinate relations as well. The purchaser and the salesperson, or two companies in a merger transaction, can benefit from defining their goals in advance and then meeting to work out a suitable joint agreement. There are usually six major steps in reaching an agreement.

1. *Define your own objectives before you go to negotiate.*

Start by listing your own long-term purposes and some strategic guidelines for getting to them. Then narrow those mission statements down to specific objectives for the immediate period ahead. One useful technique for defining objectives is to break them down into four major categories:

a. *What are the ordinary and routine things* that should be obtained. This could include regular job duties in MBO discussions. In other transactions it could include some of the ordinary commercial practices in business dealings, such as billing methods, vouchers, records, verifications, and warranty practices. Such things are usually taken for granted, and make an easy area of early agreement in negotiations.

b. *Identify what special problems exist* or can be predicted which must be solved in negotiations. In one construction contract in New York the contractor, who was an Orthodex Jew, felt strongly that his crew should not have to work on the high holy days which would occur in the midst of the contract. He made this one of his conditions of agreement, and because he negotiated openly he was able to arrange time off for those members of his crew who wished to observe those days. In a prior job he had been confronted with an enraged architect and client who had called him at home to demand that he "get his crew back on the job immediately" when it was discovered that they were absent.

Other problems include special working conditions, personal matters which could affect the relationship sometime in the future, or the provision of special amenities which would be needed in the execution of the agreement. At the same time, the other side might have special problems which they wish to have spelled out in the final agreement, thus avoiding misunderstanding or charges of betrayal and breach of agreement.

The parents of a married son found that their daughter-in-law often brought up heated complaints which led to family discord. The wise father decided to hold open negotiations. "You kids write down what you expect of us, and we will write down what we expect of you, and we'll have a family discussion to negotiate our differences." The result was most salutary. Mother agreed to quit harping at her son's hair length which his wife had chosen and supported. The kids, on their part, agreed to quit removing major appliances and furniture from the parents' house without consent. Each time a discord followed after that, a new negotiating session was called, plans and objectives defined, and the differences clarified.

c. *What problems would you like to solve?* This third category of personal objectives which you should define before entering the negotiating meeting is to define your problems which might be resolved. This is often the whole reason for negotiating. Something has gone awry, is varying from normal, or is causing you some discomfort, and thus comprises a problem. The best way to define a problem is as "a deviation from a standard." The normal course of events is disrupted because of the behavior of some other persons or group. Negotiation is a sensible way of tackling the situation, but first you spell out the problems. Ask yourself two questions:

1. What are the *present facts* of the situation as it exists?
2. What *objective* or ideal would I like to see ensue as a result of the negotiations?

The problem thus is the difference between the present and the desired, and how to move things to produce the desired. Finding the means of moving others is the essence of problem solving.

On a narrow street in New York two cars were caught in an impasse. An open parking place had been spotted by two drivers at the same time. One hastily backed into it part way. Neither would move. Traffic was being tied up, and despite shouted admonitions back and forth, neither would budge. One of New York's Finest strolled along and surveyed the situation. The policeman asked each to move and each refused. The policeman approached the driver with the tail of his car stuck into the space and reached into his pocket. The driver, fearing a ticket, eyed him warily. The policeman took out a coin and said, "Call it." The driver defiantly said, "Heads." The policeman flipped the coin and displayed a clear tails in the palm of his hand. The driver shrugged, said "Damn," and moved on. The policeman had identified the present situation, knew what was desired, and produced a Solomon-like way of resolving the problem.

Remember, you haven't defined the problem as an objective unless you have answered both questions: the present and the desired states.

d. *Innovative objectives.* The fourth category of objectives you should define before you enter into negotiation is what new things you might wish to accomplish. You may want to introduce a new plan, a changed system, a better way, a cheaper path, a faster route, a safe method, or something that would introduce greater dignity to life. This means that the present methods aren't good enough and you can't stand for the status quo. Define what the overall end result might be. Then define what *stages* will be necessary to get you progressing toward that final result, and negotiate the change one step at a time.

An upper-level manager was well known to his subordinates to be a negative person who habitually challenged every new idea or change which he hadn't thought of. One day the manager of the shipping department had a bright idea for a new packing machine. In order to make room for cartons and supplies, he was struck with the great idea that the machine should not be bolted to the floor, but should be suspended from the ceiling, leaving the space beneath free for other uses. He knew that if he suggested the idea to his negative-thinking boss he would be subjected to negative comments and derision. After some thought he planned his tactic for negotiating the innovation. He plowed into the boss's office and proposed:

"You know that new machine? The manufacturer came up with a really screwy idea which I knew you would not like, so I told him to get lost, that he was nuts, and that you wouldn't approve such a nutty scheme. He suggested we suspend the thing from the ceiling firmly with an angle iron frame to leave room for materials. I told him to get lost with his nutty schemes, that you didn't go for things like that."

"Who authorized you to speak for me? I think it was a great idea, and that is exactly what I want done. You have that damn machine installed on the ceiling and quit being such a wise guy." Which is of course exactly what the subordinate wanted in the first place.

2. *Find out what the other side's wants and needs really are.*

A little detective work about the other party is sound preliminary work to negotiating, especially if you can find something he wants, and even better if you can find something he needs. A salesman of office appliances was planning his presentation of a new line of office equipment to a corporate customer. Other firms were also in the running. Rather than going in cold with a standard pitch, he hung out in the cafeteria and struck up a conversation with some employees. In the process he discovered that the division in need of the new equipment had strict instructions to cut back on labor cost, and its budget for wages had been reduced by fifteen percent. He did some fast paperwork, and in his presentation hammered hard on the labor-saving features of his equipment. He showed how it could produce more work with less help, and suggested that attrition would take care of any layoffs. While competitors stressed features and benefits, they said little about the key want and need of the buyer. The salesman who attacked the want and need relentlessly, and even gave the names of other firms who had produced such savings who could be called for a reference, walked away with the order. Other salespeople stressed price, service, and maintenance factors, all of which were important to the customer but didn't fill his primary need and want.

If the customer is long on cash, stressing such savings won't have the same appeal as something that hits directly at wants and needs. For some it may be keeping up with a detested competitor. For others it may be price alone. For others it will be service. Picking the want and need is finding the vulnerable spot to stress in negotiation.

A movie film company needing a mansion for a set worked out the rental of a large house owned by a company president. When they learned that his daughter was a budding actress, they asked him if he wished to suggest persons who might take part in the movie. To his delight they quickly accepted when he humbly proposed his daughter, who had aspirations as an actress. The bargain was struck, and the executive went on a trip to Europe during the time of the shooting. Due to weather and other delays, upon his return the company hadn't completed shooting and needed to remain around for another week. In negotiating the extension of time, their approach wasn't to bemoan their own problems. Rather, the producer declared joyously; "Your daughter has been a great success and we would like to enlarge her part in the film to supporting actress rather than bit player." The request for a week's extension was granted without incident.

3. *Anticipate the form of resistance.*

Professor Bob Marx of Western Washington University describes what he calls a "relapse prevention" strategy. In brief, it proposes that before you go ahead with something you want to effect, always expect that there will be a relapse or setback. Try to figure out what it will be, when it will occur, and what your response will be. Alcoholics who join a group to dry them out such as Alcoholics Anonymous usually make some early progress, and then fall off the wagon in a drinking bout which may be a single relapse. If the counselor has a relapse prevention strategy, he warns the client in advance that relapses will occur, and they work out a rebound plan together. Without such a relapse strategy,

Marx proposes, many fine programs break down because of failure to be ready with remedial action.

Negotiations likewise may go swimmingly for a while, then get hung up on some small item which wasn't foreseen. Such relapses can kill the whole deal and produce losing decisions. Many a boss at goal-setting time has singled out his or her highest-performing employee to try for that extra push which would get a need solved for the firm. But there arrives a breaking point when the least little criticism, the final tiny shove, sends that best employee out the door into the hands of a competitor. Learning to anticipate and watch for these signals, and to build a relapse prevention stretegy for the time it happens, is sensible strategy for the boss.

Of course, not every form of setback and resistance can be anticipated, but here is a formula which can help cope with such resistance when it occurs:

a. When the resistance appears, don't respond too quickly if it appears to be major. Listen fully to the other side. Then show that you understand, by restating what they have said in your own words. Saying "I understand what you are saying" or "I understand what your problem is" will make your own response more civil and acceptable to the other side.

b. Treat the resistance as a want or need that the other side is expressing, which your planning hadn't anticipated.

c. Then try to find a way to meet that need at the same time as you achieve the substance of your own. You may not be able to make a horse drink, but you can make it thirsty. In Australia there is a child's verse which fits here:

> Most of life is froth and bubble,
> Some things stand out like stone.
> Understanding of another's trouble
> And courage in your own.

4. *Present your plans to get a Yes response early.*

In seeking a major objective it is most unlikely that you will achieve every goal. It is, however, important to make your first suggestion something that stands a surefire chance of being accepted. Throughout the negotiations, you want to get as many "yeses" out of the other side as possible, but especially at the beginning. It makes the prospect of an ultimate settlement tangible and real to the other side. Seek to define common areas of agreement and get the other side to agree that that is indeed what they want. In a cold war, both sides want to avoid all-out war. In labor relations, both sides probably want to arrive at an agreement without high costs to either side. In a marital dispute, both sides want to be happy. Defining the common objective clearly and without chance of disagreement starts things on a productive foot. In labor arbitration, the first step the arbitrator takes is to get an agreement on "what is the issue?" After this is agreed, each party can proceed with its case.

A passenger arrives on the last flight into Syracuse, New York, about 1:00 a.m. He needs transportation to Ithaca and there is but one cab standing outside the station. No other passengers want to hire the cab, but take off in their own cars. Approaching the cab, the passenger might ask, "How much do you want to take me to Ithaca?" or even worse, might say, "I *have* to get to Ithaca, how much do you want?" This would start a price war upward from ordinary flat rate fares. A better tactic would be to open with, "You need a good cash fare to end your night, and no one will be in after this plane. I want to go to Ithaca. We should find some figure that will be suitable to both of us, don't you agree?" You'll then learn the book rate, and then can start working down from there. You might even suggest, "I'll bet that you can beat the price of a rental car, can't you?"

5. *Develop a sense of progress toward your goals with the other side.*

It's important in working toward your objectives to give the other side the distinct impression that progress is being made and that there is indeed light at the end of the tunnel. This will make overcoming future obstacles easier. Here are some ways in which you can create such an impression:

a. From time to time in the midst of heated disagreements, summarize the agreements previously arrived at. This produces a realization that not everything is dispute and discord, and the sessions are moving onward.

b. Restate back things that the other person has said which he now seems to be contradicting. "But this morning you were really quite agreeable to that point ..." This can keep negotiations from sliding backward and rehashing old disputes already settled.

c. In team bargaining, if one person on the opposing team seems to have softened, appeal to the intractable one with the less intractable one's view. "As Joe, who is your own expert, puts it, I think we are in agreement on this point."

d. Watch the clock and remind people of how much time they have invested in the negotiations, and point out that only a few remaining issues stand in the way of an agreement. "You suggest ninety and I suggest one hundred, and we seem to be stuck, but I think we have made fine progress to come this close. I also suspect that between our two positions there is a number we can both agree on, since we have come so far."

e. Appeal to absent third parties' interests as a basis for moving toward the goal. A company president was unable to meet a loan payment, and the bank officer in charge of his account called him in and announced that he was calling the loan, which would wipe out the firm. "Now, Bill," the president said, "we have been good for each other over the years and I think we can work out a new arrangement for this loan. After all, you approved it and sent it before your loan committee, and I don't think you really want to go explain to them how you made this bad loan, when you could avoid it by stretching out the payments and refinancing the deal. They are interested in getting their loan repaid, not in running me out of business, throwing my employees out on the street, and you aren't too happy about getting your reputation as a lending officer tarred with a bad loan. Don't you agree?"

6. *Objectives are the key to agreement.*

Each party brings objectives to the negotiating table whether they are clearly defined or not. It is sound strategy to define your objectives clearly, formally, and perhaps in writing before you begin. Keeping them out of the hands of the other side is essential, of course, unless you are one of those devious types who leaves false papers around for the other side to steal and thus be sandbagged.

William Usery, onetime head of the Federal Mediation and Conci - iation Service, found that the use of objectives was indeed a key vehic e for settlements of tough labor cases. Starting with the hard-bitten forestry unions and employers, he introduced a system called "relations by objectives" to produce agreement. Dr. Reed Richardson, Industrial Relations Professor at the University of Utah, has written a whole book on *Collective Bargaining by Objectives,* with some heartening results in actual labor disputes.

Each side agrees to go caucus and prepare their objectives, and return to the table. If they have sufficient confidence in the mediator, they might even reveal their list of objectives to him or her in confidence, which arms the mediator for creative suggestions to meet the needs of each party. Objectives are thus ultimately what determine the resolution.

PART II
THE MAJOR FACTORS IN SUCCESSFUL NEGOTIATIONS

Every human benefit and enjoyment, every virtue, every prudent
act is founded on barter and compromise. Each party recognizes
the right of the other party to be in negotiation on an equal foot-
ing. He that wrestles with us strengthens our nerves and sharp-
ens our skills. Our antagonist is our helper.
—EDMUND BURKE

The following eight chapters discuss the four major factors which are present in negotiations—the chronic and permanent elements of the process. These four factors constitute your agenda for managing by negotiation. They are the four honest serving tools, the cornerstone of the building, the four horsemen of successful negotiations.

How these four relate to one another in achieving agreement satisfactory to both parties is perhaps best described as an *equilibrium*. This is represented in Fig. 1, which depicts three billiard balls suspended in a bowl which is precisely shaped and of the exact size to suspend the three balls in balance with one another. The bowl in which the negotiations occur is *planning*. It is planning which shapes the dimensions, form, and context of the negotiations. The remaining three elements all share equal weight in determining the outcome. These three elements are *power, skill,* and *timing,* each of which is equally important in determining whether the final outcome is successful. To move one is to move the other two.

Strategic planning establishes the limits of control which the parties have over the process and the final results. It determines the standards

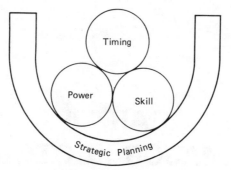

Figure 1. The Factors in Negotiation.

of conduct, policy, legal constraints, and customs within which the bargaining occurs, and the tolerances to be observed by the parties.

Power is the amount of sanction or resources which a party can exert. It may be the power to fire and hire as with a boss, the power to buy or not to buy, the power to spend or not to spend, the power to give or to withhold something. It may be economic, social, political, or administrative power. Power may be offset by adeptness, skill, and agility, but it is not reduced, merely held at bay.

Skill is what is carried to the negotiations by the individual negotiators. It is their verbal, intellectual, political, social, and psychological skills of bargaining. A wise, witty, and competent bargainer may defeat the ponderously rich or powerful on occasion.

Timing is made up of the continuity and time-phasing of the elements of negotiation and how they are deployed.

To have merely one or two of these ingredients makes you helpless in negotiations before the adversary who has all three. The person of greater resources and power, with rich personal skills in bargaining, and with a deft sense of timing will surely emerge with the best of the bargain if the context and strategic plans have been sensibly and prudently managed.

In this part of the book we will devote a chapter to each of these elements, with more than one chapter devoted to the skills of negotiation. Weak positions can be parlayed into great gains through finding the weakest element in the other side. Persuasion may offset ownership of the dollars. Giving concessions in one area may win stronger positions in others. Let's look at the four elements in some details.

5
Finding the Strategic Edge—Planning for Negotiation

An old barroom joke tells of the man who went to a favorite neighborhood bar every day with his dog, ordered a round of drinks, opened a chess board, set up the chess pieces, and played chess with his dog for the whole afternoon. One day a stranger came in and marveled at the sight. "This is fantastic," he said, "can that dog really play chess?"

"Oh, he's not so hot, I beat him three out of five games," said the dog's owner. We can presume, then, that one should never expect perfection.

Even the most powerful may be outwitted. Even the cleverest debater may find that the opposition is armed with fists and clubs which force a hasty retreat. No one can expect perfection and hope to win every issue every time in every negotiation. But through planning you might do better.

Negotiations can be approached with a somewhat similar mental set. There are negotiations that you win which you should have avoided in the first place. One day you come upon a couple of kids with a lemonade stand. By hard negotiation you beat them down to half price. Sure, it proves you are a better negotiator than the kids, but it also shows that you are a cheapskate or worse. Your skills, your power, and your timing were perfect. You arrived just when they were discouraged, since nobody had passed by for over an hour and they were getting worried. You won, but you lost as much.

There are times when to negotiate at all means that you lose.

In the case of your chiseling the kids, both sides lost. The kids didn't cover the cost of lemons and sugar, and you proved to the world that you are a petty chiseler, which reputation you don't like. The moral here, of course, is that the first step in planning for negotiating is to

decide whether you are dealing with an issue which should be negotiated or handled by some other method.

A student in one of our classes came from an upper-class family in
Westchester County, New York. "In my family we always pay the price
that is asked, we don't stoop to negotiation." This does quite a lot for
her family, which is very well-heeled. They can engage in conspicuous
consumption. They live in a world where evidence of having money is
more important than sharpness of wit or successful dealing, and the free
spending of it is evidence of having a lot of it. They always shop in the
most expensive stores, buy the most ostentatious cars rather than the
most gas-efficient, and wear clothes with labels which indicate that they
are stylish rather than useful and sturdy. Even when this girl wore den-
ims which cost $4.95 to produce, she paid $85 for them because the
name of a stylish designer was sewn on the rump.

If you are a Rockefeller and in the main line of inheritance, you don't
negotiate many deals at the personal level. You do, however, negotiate
hard if you own the biggest bank in the country and must negotiate like
an Oriental rug merchant with Arabs about loans, discounts, interest
rates, terms of repayment, and the like. Undoubtedly this young lady
could live in a nonnegotiated world because somewhere in the background her father, grandfather, or other family member had done some
sharp negotiating to make all the money needed to protect his family's
personal lives from the real world.

The strategic thinking that goes on before you use negotiations as a
tool of life is a three-part cycle. First you *set goals,* then you *execute*
your plan, then you *review* it. You define goals in order to know your
direction, and the character of your strategy. You review during negotiation and after it is over to see how you have done and to make adjust-
ments for next time.

Remember that we are talking about strategic planning for long-
range objectives, not just planning for a one-shot session. In the rest of
this chapter we will draw back and view the whole gamut of negotiations which you engage in, not just how to win that single session.
Another way of putting it is that strategy deals with doing the right
things, tactics with doing things right. It would be foolish to do the
wrong things even though you do them efficiently. Strategic planning
aims at changing the character and direction of the whole process of
negotiation across all of your affairs, not just winning a battle only to
lose the war. Strategic management has these characteristics.

a. It deals with long-range questions, usually of a multi-year duration.

b. It sees all of the elements, not just those that occur in individual bargaining.

c. It aims at long-run success, not just immediate victory. This is in fact a distinctive characteristic of this book. Other books have stressed quite well the factors which make for success in specific bargaining situations. In this part we will draw back and take a longer-range view of the strategy called negotiation.

OBJECTIVES: THE FIRST STEP

The first stage of the planning cycle (which you remember is designed to produce control of the process) is to define your *goals*. Such goals entail strategic objectives first, then specific tactical weapons to be chosen. Strategic objectives are long-term in character. Will the matter be negotiated at all, or immediately, or at some later time? There may be times when the goal is so clear that negotiation is not worthy of consideration.

Is anything nonnegotiable?

A handsome cad admires your beautiful and faithful wife. Being both unscrupulous and unendingly brash, he approaches you with the proposition that you share her favors. Or, to avoid being sexist, let's look at it from the other side. You are the happy wife of an adoring, wealthy, handsome, thoughtful, and sensitive husband. A local doxy of indisputable beauty approaches you and proposes that she would like to arrange a split schedule of his time and attention. Each of these outrageously nervy persons proposes further that they are perfectly willing to be reasonable, and would like to start immediately in negotiating the details.

If you even entertain the thought of negotiating, you are being a fool. This is the kind of case in which any negotiation at all is a loss situation. Your only possible alternative is to send the wretched person packing, without violence if possible, but by force if necessary.

There are two classes of nonnegotiable issues. The first class are merely called nonnegotiable as a tactical step in negotiations which you know will go on, when you haven't a very strong case but you really hope to win. *Stating nonnegotiability as a tactic* usually consists of making impossible demands which will infuriate the other side. If you use this as a tactic, there are some things you can do which will make it work better:

1. You can talk off-the-record to the other side. "Actually, I am not as dismayed at your demands as it might seem. You see, she can't cook, won't make the bed, spends all her time at the TV watching soaps, and has a head full of oatmeal. But I have to say no for the record."

2. You can explain why. "I can understand your position, but unfortunately I have this terrible crush on him and couldn't live without the big hunk."

3. You can change the topic to something negotiable. "Of course I can't consider your suggestion, but my wife and I know a very fine rich widow who would love to meet an interesting and audacious man like you."

If on the other hand the *issue truly is nonnegotiable* and your main goal is to chop off all contact permanently, immediately, and emphatically, you must employ other strategies.

1. You blow up. "If you aren't out of here in two seconds I will turn loose Harriet, that Doberman pinscher over there, on you, and she will make mincemeat of your lovely shape."

2. You can go public and scream bloody murder. "Help, this man is accosting me. Somebody call a cop." Make a citizen's arrest, call a press conference, take a full-page ad in *The New York Times*.

3. Call a strike, go to war with an unannounced attack, or sue. The Japanese attack at Pearl Harbor in 1941 was clear evidence that the issues were no longer negotiable.

4. If the issue is genuinely nonnegotiable, then don't negotiate even a little bit. If you give the impression that you are merely using nonnegotiability as a tactic, the other side will continue to seek a chink in your plan. An old tale tells of a man who sat down on a bus next to a young lady and reached out and took her hand. She was startled, but she saw that he was young, well-dressed, and very attractive. "Sir," she said, "if you don't release my hand by the time we have arrived at the end of the line I will inform the driver of your wholly unwanted attentions." They were married six months later.

The first step in planning and defining objectives, then, is deciding if negotiations are for you in the case at hand.

Should you consider arbitration?

A sensible strategy when the relationship is intended to be ongoing and permanent is to include an arbitration clause in every contract. This is different from ordinary negotiation, but has some important resemblances and should be considered as part of your strategic planning armamentarium for negotiation.

Arbitration means that when two parties can't agree on something of interest to both, or when one party's rights are being trampled by the other, they resolve the dispute by submitting the issue to a third party who is agreeable to both sides. Usually this third party is chosen from a list of possible names maintained by some neutral body such as the American Arbitration Association. The candidates for arbitrator are ranked by the parties, and the most acceptable one is chosen. Having agreed in advance to submit the issue, the parties also must agree to abide by the decision of the arbitrator, whose decision will be final and binding, and enforceable in court.

The arbitrator calls the meeting and often provides the neutral ground for the hearing. He or she then defines the issue, hears the evidence from both sides, and issues an award quickly. In labor arbitration this award is usually produced within thirty days of the completion of the hearing. In commercial arbitration it may take longer, but is usually far faster than the courts. It doesn't entail heavy legal expense, is quick, and doesn't require the formal rules of evidence that a court might. It is a common-sense and relatively rapid way of resolving issues in dispute. How should you incorporate arbitration in your strategy for negotiating with others?

1. Build an arbitration clause into all of your commercial and labor contracts, providing that any disagreement which the parties can't resolve after a fair trial at negotiations will be submitted to an arbitrator.

2. Choose the common contract language which is provided by most neutral bodies such as AAA and which is approved in law in most states as a legally binding part of the contract.

3. It is better to stick to issues involving *rights* of the parties rather than *interests*. This means that if a contract exists and something arises which isn't all that clear in the language of the contract, you arbitrate it. But if the question is one involving the content of the contract at

reopening time, such as wage hours or conditions of work, you avoid arbitration and stick with straight head-to-head negotiations and bargaining. It's not sensible to turn your interests over to a third party who hasn't a personal interest in the outcome. The questions of rights under an agreement lend themselves extremely well to such a process.

BASE YOUR PLANNING ON FACTS

While rhetoric and persuasion are important, the basic building block in negotiation is a sound factual base. Have statistics available, and as you enter negotiations, all relevant facts should be marshaled, organized, and studied, and the meanings teased out of them. Psychologist Tom Gilbert differentiates between information and data. *Data,* he says, is like a haystack, lots of individual straws of varying lengths pointing in all directions. *Information* on the other hand is like a needle, it has an eye and a point and is going someplace and dragging a thread behind it. The only way to handle data is with a pitchfork, and in large bundles. You'd do better to use information than data, facts than rhetoric. This doesn't mean you won't use the latter, but it's more comfortable and offers a better chance of winning if you are solidly fact-based in your prior planning.

Where, then, is the needle rather than the bale of straw in planning for negotiation? Just refer back to the model—you know, the bowl with the three billiard balls inside representing power, skill, and timing. The following check lists certainly don't cover every question but they illustrate how to size up your negotiation situation strategically:

1. *Facts about your power—balance with the other side.*

> Is the other side wealthier?
> Is it longer on cash immediately available?
> Does it have more people?
> Does it have special talent on tap such as lawyers, or scientists?
> Do they have political connections which will help them?
> Are they widely respected and admired?
> Do they have access to media and public communications?

To construct a more complete fact base for planning, study Chap. 6 on power in negotiations and assess your own power as it matches against that of the other side. For example, you are a small retailer with limited capital and you are approached by a powerful union which proposes that you agree to a collective bargaining agreement with the union as representative of your employees. They allude to some highly undesirable consequences to your business if you refuse. You might find that your supplier will refuse to deliver their products, and vague other ominous occurrences might be forthcoming. In sizing up the facts, you conclude that the balance of power with respect to certain aspects lies with the other side.

They have more money.
They have muscle.
They have numbers of people to throw into a battle.
They have a power to affect your friends and suppliers.
They could last longer than you in any version of battle.

On the other hand, as you size up your own power base factually, you might conclude that you have certain assets. The factual study shows you that the following are in your favor:

You belong to a good trade association which helps its members.
You belong to the city chamber of commerce.
Your employees probably don't want the union.
Your customers are generally quite satisfied with you.
Your accountant can provide information on costs of options.
Your lawyer has had some labor relations experience.
The federal and state government prohibit muscle from being used.
You and the chief of police are good friends.

2. *Build upon the facts about your negotiating skills.*

One of the best ways of learning to negotiate is to take part in negotiations as a member of a team with an experienced and skilled negotiator heading operations. Lacking this, you may find your education more expensive than you ever imagined possible.

The average life of a business in this country is said to be about seven years. Most business failures occur in the early life of the business, and a large part of this early failure is due to the unconscionable expense of bargaining with suppliers, contractors, vendors, and merchants for the start-up costs of the business. Without skilled negotiating, it is almost a sure thing that novice entrepreneurs will end up paying considerably more than they should have or would have paid if they had experience in dealing and bargaining. The technical expert who starts a small firm out of his or her invention is usually unskilled in negotiating, and is soundly thrashed, skinned, and roasted by every contractor and supplier who comes along. Having plucked the hapless victim mercilessly, they will hound him endlessly to collect every last cent when he runs into cash shortages. Had the now sadder but wiser victim been more aware of his or her own limitations in negotiating, the early demise might have been averted. At least it could have been drawn out, and might even have resulted in the infant business surviving. Here are some questions you might use to assess your own negotiating experience.

- How many times have I actually negotiated in this kind of situation?
- Can I predict what will occur in the negotiations?
- Do I have some responses to the other side's moves?
- Do I know how to begin, what to do next?
- How much should I rely on experts and advisers?
- Who could I get to go on my side?

One of the advantages of reading books about negotiations such as this one, or Chet Karrass' or Herb Cohen's, is that you can get some objective assessment of your skills. Reading the book may improve your skill a bit, but it certainly won't take the place of actual negotiations. Even better would be a good course or seminar such as those offered by Gerard Nirenberg, which certainly will help you.

3. *Face the facts about your timing.*

The third and often overlooked area gathering facts in preparing for negotiation is the management of your timing. How can you handle something as vague as that? Remember you are going to start with facts.

Begin by taking out a calendar for the next year or two and start managing-by-anticipation. Scan the months ahead and identify the key dates which will occur in your dealings with others.

a. List all of the dates when contracts, leases, projects, and events will be ending which might provide an opportunity to make gains through negotiation.

For example, you conclude that the old car you have been nursing for seven years will finally have to be traded in this year. You will do far better if you plan ahead to the approximate time when you will make that transaction. You might want to time your purchase at just after the start of the new model year, and buy a *new last-year's model*. When the dealer has a showroom full of new models, but also has some new cars left over from last year, the price and fringes on the old-year cars are apt to be timed for sale, and your bargaining power is better.

b. Space your various deals so you won't get caught in several important negotiations at the same time. If, for example, you have to renew your labor contract, don't let your lease reopener come up the same week. You'll find yourself dashing from place to place and juggling two sets of facts and figures.

One large Eastern chemical company had been troubled by a series of labor contracts which left it at a competitive disadvantage. The labor relations vice president was a veteran bargainer, but he seemed to be a constant victim of union whipsawing and joint union actions which left him worse off than his competitors. A higher-paid consultant reviewed the company's practices and advised that they start staggering the closing dates of individual contracts, because the problem lay in uniform companywide closing dates of all 75 plant contracts. Over the next five to seven years the company worked hard on the timing of their contracts, and produced a year-round schedule of plant bargaining. This produced not only a more orderly schedule of negotiations for the central office, it threw more responsibility upon individual plant managers and their local labor relations managers to bargain local issues more effectively. The crisis atmosphere of bargaining which previously came around in a giant "hell month" was now a steady process which could be analyzed while it was going on.

In other cases, such as the United Auto Workers, the union strategy is to bargain and settle first with one of the Big Three before negotiating with the other two. This first firm becomes the target, and it seems customary to call a strike on this firm first to produce big gains. Once the target firm has fallen, it has been quite routine for the other two competitors to fall into line. This use of phased timing reduces the amount of work and pay lost by members, produces higher contract settlements, and permits focused efforts by the top union leadership, which would not be possible in a three-ring circus of bargaining all at once.

c. Prepare a master calendar of negotiations for one or two years ahead for your organization, or for your own personal affairs.

- After the calendar is roughed out, check it with others who might have additions or changes to suggest.
- Disseminate it widely to responsible people and ask people to prepare subcalendars to supplement it.
- Check it for deadlines which are manageable and are bunched up. If you have lined up all salary reviews to occur the same week for the whole firm, you may be placing a heavy negotiation burden upon line managers and the quality will go down. You might consider what some firms do: schedule salary reviews to come on the employee anniversary date, or on some other timephased schedule.

Most calendars have too much negotiation occurring at the same time, usually in order to fit the fiscal year. After you have prepared your negotiations schedule, look for items that could be shifted to earlier or later dates. It will help take the heat off the sessions, for bargaining under pressure increases deadline bargaining, or even worse, catch-up negotiation.

RELATE YOUR PLANS FOR NEGOTIATION TO CHANGES IN OUTSIDE CONDITIONS

In 1981 a change in the economic climate and in the relative strength of labor vs. management occurred which altered the negotiations stance of the two parties. Faced with industry trends that suggested that plants, jobs, or whole industries were threatened with elimination, employers began to press demands upon unions to reopen old contracts and accept reduced wages and benefits. Unions in automobiles, steel, rubber, newspapers, farm equipment, mining, smelting, airlines, meat packing, and railroads by the start of 1982 had accepted such give-back demands of management. Government employees, confronted with a reduction in force of federal employees, tax revolts in the states, and declining enrollments in the schools, had all conceded such give-back contract negotiations at the initiative of management.

A key element in strategic planning for negotiations in your organization must include some scanning of the environment to detect early what these influences might do to your power position, and your timing of demands. You may be able to wait out the other side when they can't afford to wait. Market information may tell you that demand for a product is declining due to changing tastes of consumers, which places your suppliers in a less enviable position. When their capacity may be standing idle, you are in a strong negotiation position to press for added services, price breaks, or other economic advantage than when you need their supplies and they are already overbooked. If you have a monopoly on a badly needed product, your bargaining strength is enhanced, and this should be documented clearly before you start any specific sessions or series of negotiations.

PLAN TO BUILD YOUR OWN SKILLS

A factual assessment of the negotiation calendar and the requirements of people to conduct negotiations will help you determine your resources in talent, time, and money to enter the future in negotiating your business problems.

a. What are your major strengths in terms of people skilled in negotiations? If you have weaknesses, what are some training or developmental actions you can take to bolster those areas?

b. How do you select the team of people to execute your negotiations? Are they chosen for their technical know-how, because they have authority to make decisions, because they have personal qualities to win, or because they are the only ones available?

c. What third parties will be involved in negotiations, as negotiators (lawyers, consultants, etc.) or as technical experts?

d. Do you have a careful plan for deploying people so that you have reserves and back-up people? You may start negotiations with agents or initiators who don't have the power to make final decisions, holding the final decisions for an absent third party who stays in the background. This will be necessary if you are thin on strong negotiating skills at all levels.

e. How well do you use status as a means of presenting a strong face to the other side? Having top people open the negotiations, defining the issues and resolving the major topics, and then leaving the technical details to lower-level people is a planned strategy in some organizations.

COPING WITH CRISIS NEGOTIATIONS

When the Iranians captured our embassy in Teheran, the U.S. public was introduced to a concept which is evidence of sound negotiation planning. Within the State Department a crisis team was formed to handle day-to-day issues as they arose during the crisis. Such a crisis contingency plan should be part of every negotiation strategic system.

An airport humor rack card suggests irreverently that "when you are up to your ass in alligators, it is sometimes difficult to remember that your objective was to drain the swamp." While this will evoke a laugh from every experienced negotiator, it also suggests that people may be overly attracted to crisis bargaining, and even when it might have been prevented they will cling to it joyously for they enjoy crises. While it makes life exciting and urgent, it does little for the successful outcome of negotiation. Alligators, if the truth be known, have inhabited swamps for some 150 million years, and have always behaved voraciously toward other mammals entering their domain. Surely if something has been going on for that long it might seem possible to develop a systematic plan for alligator protection before rushing blindly into a swamp-draining contract. Perhaps a special kind of boat, or even a subcontractor might avert the worst effects. You might even want to ask whether it is a sound objective to drain the swamp at all, or whether you might attain your goal by some other means. If no such outlet exists, then you might think about finding some jobs for the alligators which will occupy them in activities other than gobbling up your employees. You might hire them as timekeepers, talk it out with their lawyers, or simply move them to another swamp while the operation is under way.

Devising an emergency action plan is part of the planning process for negotiations. We may not be able to wholly prevent fires, but we can create well-staffed fire departments, and ask that they do some preventive inspections as well as responding to the bell when it rings.

REVISE YOUR NEGOTIATING STRATEGIC PLANS PERIODICALLY

At least annually you should haul out your long-range plans for negotiations in labor, purchasing, land and property management, management by objectives, subcontracting, claims processing, licensing, mergers and acquisitions, customer warranty claims, leases, and joint ventures, and review your strategies for each.

Remember that a five-year plan isn't one that lasts five years, but should be revised annually. Check it against your past results, changing trends, and shifts in your power, your skills, and for needed changes in timing.

Your Negotiations Planning Effectiveness

How effective are you in negotiations? Rate yourself between 0 and 100 on each of the following items. 60 is passing. Also, check five items on which you could advantageously improve your effectiveness.

	0–100 Self-Rating	Check Top 5 for Improvement
Knowing what you need and want	————	————
Knowing what you are likely to get	————	————
Knowing what the other party really needs	————	————
Knowing what the other party will give	————	————
Having necessary facts and information	————	————
Knowledge of trends	————	————
Developing your presentation	————	————
Anticipating the other party's presentation	————	————
Organizing your team	————	————
Presenting your position	————	————
Preparing to listen	————	————
Developing defense for your position	————	————
Timing of trading—getting and giving concessions	————	————
Preparing for persuasion	————	————
Developing questions	————	————
Anticipating questions	————	————
Analysis of power—yours and theirs	————	————
Development of alternatives	————	————

	0–100 Self-Rating	Check Top 5 for Improvement
Gaining respect	_____	_____
Avoiding pitfalls	_____	_____
Timing	_____	_____
Clarity of agreement	_____	_____
Overall negotiating effectiveness with individuals	_____	_____

6
How to Use Power in Negotiation

The exclusive use of force eventually raises up the forces that
destroy it.
—ANATOL RAPPOPORT

In one Western state the Junior League, a women's group, threw its
support behind a bill in the state legislature which would provide financial support for a program in the arts. Having found a legislator who
would introduce the bill, the women started a personal lobbying campaign with the membership of the legislative body. They swarmed all
over the chambers and offices of the capital, pleading with and cajoling
the members of that august body to support their bill. They were treated
with utmost courtesy, and even a certain amount of flirtatious flattery.
The bill, however, never stood a prayer of winning and was defeated by
a wide margin. The women, regrouping to assess the situation, decided
to solicit the support of other women's groups to conduct a series of
benefits, dances, cake sales, and other fund-raising events for their arts
program. The thought apparently never occurred to them to organize
their political power and punish at the polls the legislators who had
voted against their bill. Power did not seem to be part of their thought
processes at the time. The idea that they could draw on the feminist
groups in the state, organize the majority of voters, who happened to be
women, and enter a down-and-dirty political brawl and win not only
that fight but others in the future which women might want, didn't cross
their minds. They failed to realize that power establishes its own base
and that failure to use the power which is in your own hand means to
succumb to lesser power. Legislators in this case and elsewhere are
more likely to bet on winners, and attend to what power holders want.
To refuse to use power which is in your grasp means suicide in negotiation. Still, the collection and use of power is complex and not to be

employed crudely nor to excess. Power in the end is a kind of weapon which if imprudently applied poisons everyone it touches.

WHAT IS POWER AND WHERE DOES IT COME FROM?

An interviewer was surveying the attitudes of employees in a large firm. The first question was "How long have you worked here?" A diligent and hard-working employee who had once been known as a lazy loafer replied, "Since the day they threatened to fire me." Power thus has the potential to influence the behavior of others. The stubborn antagonist becomes an avid supporter. The reluctant customer becomes an eager buyer, or at least places the order. The boss who refused permission now willingly supports and endorses a proposed line of action by a subordinate.

Two social scientists, John R. P. French and Bertran Raven, propose five major sources of power:

1. *Reward power* means you have the ability to reward another for going in your direction. This may be actual, or simply a perception. It is said that Rutgers University was named after Colonel Henry Rutgers, a wealthy burger of New York, in anticipation of his generosity. Unfortunately, they named the college before the details of the grant had been worked out. After the commitment to his name had been made, however, Henry apparently decided that the *fait accompli* wasn't worth much, and his largesse consisted only of donating a large bell for the college chapel. Not only must rewards be properly timed, but once given they must be continued. This is illustrated in the story of the five-year-old whose language was taking on a distinctly salty flavor. His concerned grandmother called him in and passed him a nickel. "I am giving you this nickel so that you won't use that naughty word ever again!" The pleased youngster went off happily to spend this reward, but returned in half an hour. "Grandma, I just heard a word that is worth fifty cents," he announced.

2. *Coercive power* affects behavior through ability, real or imaginary, to punish or harm. The large, muscular individual gets his way more often than the ninety-seven-pound weakling. Even if the giant smiles and appears to be genial, people size up his potential for inflicting damage and more often than not decide to go along with his requests, even when couched in the most conciliatory and placating language. Napoleon is credited with observing that God is on the side of the army with the most battalions. When a depression occurs, the labor unions, faced

with layoffs and cutbacks, realize that their bargaining power is diminished; they are then apt to be defined by management as "reasonable." However, such influence may last only as long as the power exists. The biblical tale of Samson illustrates how the behavior of adversaries will revert back to its former ways when power is removed. Shorn of his hair, Samson was a joke.

3. *Legitimate power,* French and Raven suggest, is that which is attributed as legal and rightfully belonging to one side by another. For centuries the father was seen as the head of the family, his power delegated directly from God, in the prevailing culture of the times. This is the power of position. People have a happy willingness to concede that people in some positions have the right to give orders, which they as followers have the duty to obey. The priest, the teacher, the policeman, the judge, the elected official and his delegated subordinates have certain powers which people recognize.

It is only at special and somewhat rare times that people rebel against such legal authority. During the sixties, students defied establishment figures, but this too passed away, and by 1972 a more respectful generation had supplanted their older brothers and sisters, and college administration had become more traditional and stable. Thoreau noted that power is the basis of government, for, he observed, governments have neither wit, wisdom, nor morality but merely power. It is the command of armies and police, the power to assess and tax, the ability to send marshals to hale you into court, that produce compliance with the sovereign power of the state.

4. *Referent power,* or the power to *influence others,* is still another source and classification of power. This may be in the form of charisma or aura which can be thrown behind certain causes by individuals possessing it. Every important and visible figure draws around him a retinue of followers, admirers, and devotees who will adhere to his wishes and whims. Often the person of influence will effect sweeping changes without even making a request for action. Influention people provide models for others who copy them. When George Romney was president of American Motors, he often showed up for work as early as six a.m. This produced a whole rash of early arrivers coming in at six, even though the charismatic Mr. Romney never issued any orders that others emulate his strange hours. This kind of power is apt to make some permanent changes in others, and even after Romney went on to become governor of Michigan many at American Motors continued his early-morning habits.

5. *Expert power* is the power of knowledge. It clusters around people who have knowledge about things that most people don't have and produces deference to their behavior and wishes. This is apt to be because of the special training and education of the power holder, such as the lawyer, the surgeon, or the native guide on the hunting trip. This power is often based upon trust that the expert will abide by the rules of his profession to tell the truth. Having control of information is a form of expert power. The boss who opens the meeting with the announcement "I have here a directive from the board of directors" is wielding both positional and informational power.

The limit on such power is, of course, that it is generally restricted to the expert's area of expertise. When Linus Pauling, the Nobel laureate in physics, announced a cure for the common cold, he was roundly criticized by the experts in medicine. The executive who is an expert in finance may find that his or her judgments about art, fine wines, and politics are less persuasive.

In addition to these five sources of power, we might note some others which have been identified by other social scientists and which have a bearing on the use of power in negotiation:

- In most organizations the control of budgets and of personnel hiring and firing, promotion and demotion, are sources of power. The strong manager who wishes to exert control seeks out and grasps these two vital elements of power.
- Real power and apparent power aren't always the same thing and may rest in different people. The non-com in the army who knows the ropes may have more power than the second lieutenant who lacks experience.
- The more legitimate the power—that is, the more acceptable it is to the other side—the less resistance it generates.
- Power increases your visibility, and some people are made nervous by the glare that power generates and hence don't seek out or use power very well.
- Power, suggests R. G. H. Siu, is always based upon self-discipline—"the severe self-discipline of dedication and destiny, of great tyrant and master robber." If you can't stand this demand upon yourself, retreat to a quiet subservience, he proposes.
- The total stock of power is never really added to or subtracted from, it is merely clustered up or dispersed.

- Power behind the scenes is just as real as formal and visible power. Power brokers and undercover power groups play an important part in the negotiation process.
- Morality and ethics are the most durable sources of power. People have to believe that the other side is on the level if they are to be influenced by them. Senator William Fulbright in his book *The Arrogance of Power* suggests that an administration which is based upon power is illegitimate in the eyes of the governed. Only moral power, suggests Walter Lippmann, has the staying power to keep the powerful in office.

EIGHTEEN RULES FOR USING POWER IN NEGOTIATIONS

The objective here, of course, isn't to produce one of those "how to grab power to kick others in the teeth" books. Rather, the subject is the use of power in the negotiation process. You'll recall that power is but one of three billiard balls suspended in the cereal bowl of strategic planning to get where you would like to be through bargaining.

Here are some rules for using power effectively in negotiations:

1. *Your objective is to get others to do what you need and want.* If in the process they also get what they want, so much the better. This means you may have to shuffle interests. Find out what you want and need first. Then try to figure out what they need and want. Figure 6-1 shows how to prepare a chart to help define your objectives. First make a list of your *needs* across the lower line, rated from low to high. On the vertical line make a list of your *wants.* You can now classify your goals in the form of a portfolio of negotiating goals.

Square A. In the lower left corner are those possible demands which are low on both your need and want lists. Use these as bargaining chips, to be conceded without any serious loss.

Square B. *High wants, low needs.* These are things you would love to get for ego or some other personal reason, but which you could live okay without. Trade them, but only for some real return.

Square C. *High need value, high want.* These are where you go to the mattress, declare war, take a strike. Your company would go broke, you would be in the poorhouse, your reputation ruined if you backed down here. Stick fast and don't give up an inch without a real struggle. Try to trade off some A and B items to assure winning these.

Square D. *Low wants, high needs.* These are items you really need

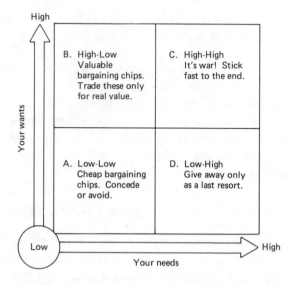

Figure 6-1. A Portfolio of Negotiator Needs and Wants.

but hate to pay the price of getting. You may have to lose some face or sacrifice personal attachments to get something you need to survive. Bargaining items which fall into this category should be clearly spelled out, and you may need third-party advice on handling them.

2. *Agreement through negotiation produces power over outsiders.* In the Taft Hartley Law, the strength of collective bargaining is recognized as superior to judgments dictated by a third party. When you can assert that an agreement has been reached which is satisfactory to the two parties in dispute, you have overcome many of the possible objections which might be raised by third parties who haven't as much interest in the outcome as the two principals. If the disputants in negotiation can agree, they will find that others will see more virtue in the course of action produced than from any other form of action plan. The world likes agreements honestly arrived at, and the power of both parties in agreement is stronger than a directed action by one or the other. The power of two is greater than the power of one.

When in Poland in 1981 the Solidarity labor party and the Communist Party were railing at each other in bitter dispute, the world watched anxiously, and even the Russians showed restraint, unlike their behavior in Hungary twenty-one years before, hoping that the two could achieve agreement without force.

3. *Power in negotiation can be real or apparent.* If you have little

power but can generate an illusion that you have a lot, the effect may be the same as having actual power. Thus, it is sensible in bargaining to attempt to create an illusion of power, which at its best is undetectable by the other side. Parading a few weapons publicly can be enhanced by some dummy displays to create an illusion of greater power. The army which builds extra campfires, or the defenders of a weak position who set off firecrackers to produce an illusion of firepower, rely upon generating this illusion. Be ready to set off your firecrackers and explosives around the perimeter if you would like to convince the other side that you have more power than you really do. If on the other hand you have genuine power, don't let the other side fall into underestimating you, unless you are setting a trap to ambush them. Power can be dangerous if it is perceived as being nonexistent by the other side, for this misperception may lead to dangerous actions which can tear a situation to shreds and reduce the world to rubble.

4. *The power of the opposing party is easily overestimated.* Many negotiators overestimate the power of the other side and spend their time waffling back and forth in front of their fortifications rather than attacking and winning the field early. The personal style and manner of the other side may bluff you, and strongly entrenched positions should always be probed and tested before you fold up and give away the farm. The best way of estimating their real strength is to use the grid chart shown in Fig. 6-1, in which you drew up your own portfolio of needs and wants.

Now try to construct a chart for the other side, and keep adding to it as they reveal their hand in negotiation.

It will look something like Figure 6-2 on p. 68.

Match each square. If you see that both of you need the same thing, agreement will be easy. If you estimate that they are huffing and puffing over one of your category A low-lows, try to get something of value (high-high) for it. The rules are simple:

- Always try to trade one of their wants or needs for one of your wants.
- *Never, never* give away a need of your own for a want of theirs.
- Remember that the deadlock will come when your needs and their are in conflict.
- Use your wants to buy as many of your needs as possible.
- Remember that it is *your needs which give them power,* and it is *their needs which give you power.*

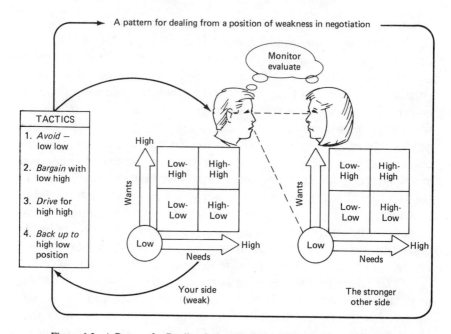

Figure 6-2. A Pattern for Dealing from a Position of Weakness in Negotiation.

5. *Exercise of power entails risks and costs.* During World War II on an island in the South Pacific an army division was due to be equipped with new vehicles for an invasion of the Philippines. The new equipment arrived and was issued by the division ordnance company to all units of the division, in exchange for the old vehicles. The division ordnance commander then asked his commanding general what should be done with the old vehicles. "Turn them in to the base ordnance company," was the reply.

The base ordnance officer, however, refused to take them, producing an obscure regulation which stated that "all equipment designated as obsolete must be surveyed and an eight page report filed for each item of equipment prior to its acceptance." The division was due to ship out for an invasion in two days, and such a monumental paper job was patently impossible. The base ordnance officer grinned gleefully at his ploy. He had apparently won his freedom from a troublesome job of receiving and storing all of those vehicles. The game failed, however. The division ordnance officer quickly sent a dozen non-coms forth on the island base to visit every imaginable kind of unit, offering free vehicles to anyone who would sign a receipt for them. Every tiny army unit, the navy, the marines, and Australians all eagerly accepted the free transportation, signed the receipts, and began happily driving around the base in their trucks, jeeps, tanks, and scout cars. With all of the used vehicles now out of their hands, and having receipts for all of them, the division departed. Just before departure, the division ordnance officer notified the base inspector general that 1,400 vehicles were running around without proper authorization. The base ordnance officer was directed to go find every one of them, and he was left with the unenviable task of spending weeks recovering all of the unauthorized vehicles. His risk had turned into a massive headache.

6. *Power changes over time.* The reason for this change is of course that people's needs change. If something was critically needed a month ago, but now is not even wanted, your power of withholding that need is worthless, for it is no longer a need. When a need stops being a need, it reduces the power of the person holding it. The gasoline retailer was in a position of power in 1973 and again in 1979 when supplies were short and rationing was installed in many states. By 1981 when a surplus existed, price controls were removed, and conservation started to work, the gas retailers found they not only had no power over customers but even had to engage in price cutting, giving away premiums, and staying open longer hours in order to sell their excess stocks. Don't presume that the source of your power this year will remain a source of power forever. Each time you enter negotiations you need to rework your needs-wants portfolio, and that of your adversary.

7. *Specific power is often more important than general power.* An American lady whose family was stationed in Manila went out into the country to purchase eggs. She found that the egg farmer was asking ten pesos per dozen. She protested, "But you have always delivered them to my house in Manila for seven pesos." "That's true, lady," replied the farmer. "But when I go to Manila to sell eggs, I need the money. When you come out to the country, it's because you need eggs." The only saloon in town can serve smaller shots and cheaper brands at higher prices than if fifty saloons lined the streets. Specific power may be positional, or it may be because of the specific timing requirements of the wants. A theater ticket has much more value when you have traveled far to come to town to see that specific show than if you are a resident and can choose your night for attending, or if you aren't all that turned on by a specific show.

8. *Time is power.* As the chapter on timing will reveal in more detail, the ability to wait out the other side is an important ingredient in fixing the focus of power. The small supplier who needs immediate cash is more susceptible to being squeezed on price, service, and quality when dealing with a giant firm's purchasing department than a large firm which has millions in cash sitting around in the bank. Similarly, the firm which has no immediate cash-flow problems can compete better for government contracts where the payment schedule is very slow. The accounts receivable are an asset on their books which they can carry far better than the individual or small contractor who must pay the help, and pay his own suppliers in ten days or less.

9. *Power is relative and seldom complete.* The power to muscle others may not be exercised to its utmost in most cases. There may be laws, customs, and absent third parties who must be considered. Old John D. Rockefeller Senior was a master of manipulation of railroad rates and used this control to run competitors out of business, extort fierce demands on suppliers and customers, and wield the power of size and monopoly without mercy. In the end, however, the Standard Oil empire was broken up by an overwhelming public outcry at the concentration of power in a single person. The Sherman and Clayton antitrust laws often are used as the basis for one firm filing a sizable law suit against another firm for restraint of trade and monopolistic practices. It is possible to negotiate too hard.

10. *Rewards are a source of power.* When the boss has control over pay raises, promotions, and assignments, and has the ability to make a subordinate personally prosperous, it colors the terms of agreements about objectives. In one large auto firm the general manager made it a practice to remind his subordinates, "I won't tell you what objectives to set for your department, but please remember who will be making the decisions on bonus allocations at the end of this year." Few subordinates had sufficient nobility of character to defy such a crass and profane approach. They went back and worked up the numbers to come out closer to those which would please the boss.

Rewards, however, have a motivating effect and are a source of power only as long as they continue. Many a firm which installed profit-sharing plans found that a letdown occurred in those years when their profits fell rapidly. Performance was disproportionately worse than if the rewards for success had not been so generous in the past. Intangible rewards such as praise and recognition likewise require a steady course if they are to continue to have a beneficial effect and comprise a useful source of power. Using recognition should be done sparingly and evenly rather than wantonly and wildly. Issuing profuse thanks for a minor and routine achievement robs the reward felt by the subordinate of much of its effect, and won't produce the large gains which should produce large gobs of rocognition for great attainments.

11. *Fear of punishment is a source of power.* If the other side has the power to make you feel pain for not cooperating or conceding, they have power over you. While this is apparent in many boss-subordinate situations, it is equally true in commercial and labor transactions. It has serious limits, however. On a late night in Dallas a fast-talking Yankee traveler showed up at a Holiday Inn and demanded a room. The desk clerk politely told the guest that they were all filled up. The customer launched into a tirade, berating the clerk, the hotel, and the corporation. The clerk remained calm and polite. Finally the customer played what he hoped was trump. "This slip is a guaranteed late arrival. Now let's see you find that room you just told me you don't have." The clerk quietly examined the slip and replied, "I regret to say, sir, that this reservation is for another Holiday Inn forty miles from here. You have come to the wrong hotel." The customer then paid fifty dollars for a cab ride to the right hotel. All of which shows that using the fear of punishment as a means of negotiation can backfire unless you have the stuff to back it up.

12. *Resources are the best form of power creation.* The owner of a valuable resource has the most persuasive basis for power and may use it more freely than other forms of power. Having control of a scarce raw material, being in a strong cash position, or having plenty of manpower and talent available provides a real basis of power that can only be coped with through conciliation, persuasion, and negotiating skill. If the holder of the strongest resource wishes to hold out, and has the will to do so, the other side must lose.

13. *Information, knowledge, and technology contribute to power.* In a technological world the technologist has power. In the early kibbutzim in Israel it was an article of faith and a central purpose of the community that all people would be equal in all things. The work would be divided equally, past education and social status notwithstanding. They quickly learned, however, that when a child was stricken with appendicitis, or a member broke a limb, that the physician in the commune, as the only one who knew how to take effective remedial action, held all

the power necessary to command resources, direct others, and be relieved of cleaning the stables that day. Perfect equality can exist in a group only when all are equally ignorant. Infuse different levels of knowledge and skill, and power begins to cluster up in those who have it.

In the James M. Barrie play *The Admirable Crichton* a wealthy family is stranded on a desert isle. The only member of the group who knew how to do things such as cook, light a fire, and arrange shelter was Crichton the butler. While back in England he had been merely a servant, on the island he was the boss, for his knowledge made him the source of life for the rest. Thus, it isn't merely higher levels of education which comprise this knowledge-based power source, but any kind of knowledge which the others don't have and which they need.

14. *Initiative is a source of power.* A small dog fell through the ice on the campus pond at Amherst one spring day. While hundreds of anguished students stood about bewailing the fate of the helpless pet struggling in the icy water, one person, a marketing professor named Mary Barber, quickly waded into the icy water, breaking ice as she went, grasped the dog by the scruff of the neck, and carried it to shore. Barking orders, she soon had students rushing to the dorm for towels, workmen producing ropes to block off the entrance to the pond, and faculty carrying her briefcase. Spotting a high official in the crowd, she ordered, "Provost, you call my dean and tell him I won't be at the curriculum committee meeting this afternoon." The startled provost, a very high figure, rushed off to obey the orders of this intrepid heroine without question.

People who are willing to make bold decisions, assuming risks that the more timorous are fearful of doing, collect a kind of power that the average member of the crowd doesn't acquire. We might divide the world into the deciders and the drifters, and the deciders have a certain amount of power which is directly attributable to their decisiveness. The simple soldier who leads the charge can shout commands to others, and they often will obey. Often the decisiveness is not based upon a belief in assurance of success, but merely a propensity for taking charge, with the confidence that it will produce compliance in others. Of course there are occasions in which the risks are too high and the hero fails. Knowing when to act assertively and decisively is an art. The willingness to make big commitments of any kind is a potent contributor to power.

15. *Having options is a source of power.* The person with the largest

number of options has an advantage over the person who has but one. Robert McNamara, onetime president of Ford, former Secretary of Defense, and president of the World Bank, has a considerable reputation as a decision maker who gets his way. High in his list of techniques is the constant generation of many options. He realizes that having options gives you strength over those with few options. Your decisions, whether in buying a house, picking a spouse, negotiating your job responsibility, or choosing a college to attend, are all certain to be better decisions if you have generated numerous options. The student who has been accepted by both Harvard and Cornell stands a better chance of being admitted to a lesser college than the student who has but one acceptance, at Podunk.

If ten men want to marry the same girl, her negotiating power in making the final choice is quite favorable. If ten companies are bidding for a contract, the purchaser has considerable power in exacting service add-ons, favorable prices and terms of payment, and desirable delivery schedules. Before you enter negotiations, it is eminently sensible to create as many alternatives as possible to those things you know the other side will be demanding.

16. *Loyalty is a source of power.* The airline traveler who shows a million-mile tag on his luggage gets more attention and assistance than the youngster who is patently a novice at travel. Purchasers, like most of us, tend to be habitual in many of their relationships with vendors, and will be more disposed to go along with a proven performer than a new one for the bulk of their buying.

The long-service employee has more clout with the boss in amending his or her proposed goals than the person fresh out of college. Past contriutions have a way of being money in the bank. The bank teller of thirty years who is caught in a small defalcation will not be prosecuted—in contrast with the freshly hired young beginner, who is apt to be made an example. The ten-year-old dog will be forgiven some lapses in polite behavior around the house, while the pup will be severely punished for a similar failure. Stressing loyalty and time enjoyed in a comfortable relationship is a most useful negotiating source of power.

Cronyism is scornfully denounced, especially by those who are not part of the crony group. Every President of the United States has found that having some loyal and trusted associates close to him made the pressures of the job more tolerable. Often it is these same cronies who engage in various wrongful practices, but it is usually done with impunity, and even when they are caught red-handed they often escape with a reluctant farewell and expression of regret, plus some quiet assistance in placement in a comfortable new spot. If you can invoke cronyism, you may offset numerous other weaknesses in bargaining position.

17. *Prestige and personal charm are sources of power.* When Ronald Reagan became president he produced in his early days an almost over-powering display of this principle. He charmed the Congress, even the Democratic side, with his personal warmth, style, and grace in social relations.

Knowing this principle, however, doesn't automatically make it available to all. Some people are naturally or by long training and experience warm and personable. Others are cold and must appear cold, aloof, and unsympathetic. It is therefore a mistake for a person who is clearly the latter to try to affect the former, for such behavior must surely be seen as stilted, affected, and phony. The cardinal rule here calls for some self-knowledge and adherence to three rules:

a. *Know yourself.* If you have charm and warmth, you can use it, but if you don't, you can't, and therefore must find some other strength which is uniquely yours. Everyone has something they do best. Being a constant and consistent person, even a constant ogre, is better than being a poor actor. Knowing your own special qualities is the first step.

b. *Like yourself.* As one wag has put it, "I may not be perfect but there are parts of me that are excellent." you should find those parts of you which are excellent and lean heavily on these and not try to be excellent in things which you can never excel in. Rather, you can work harder to avoid the possible adverse effects of those less excellent features and work freely upon your best qualities.

c. *Be yourself.* Act out your own self in negotiations. If you are silent and reserved, use that well. If you are verbal and effusive and do it well, make that your power point. Talk them under the table. You will be more comfortable, free from the stress that comes with carrying an unnatural pose.

One day in 1864, it is reported, some ladies from Boston visited President Lincoln to complain about General Ulysses S. Grant. His heavy drinking was their major complaint, but they also cited his lack of manners, unkempt appearance, and brusque personality. Lincoln listened calmly, then asked, "Ladies, do you know what kind of whisky he drinks? I would like to buy a case for my other generals. I can't spare this man. He fights." It was true that Grant drank, smoked foul cigars, got ashes on his uniform, his beard was unkempt and his uniforms sloppy. But he and Lincoln ignored those features and concentrated upon his dogged strength at pushing ahead however formidable the obstacles, heavy the casualties, and brilliant the Confederate Army commanders. He played his strengths and didn't try to be a dazzling figure. Other generals such as Sheridan were more picturesque. Clad in European made uniforms, always riding a white horse, waving a shiny saber, Sheridan was a picture-book general, exuding charm and charisma. His shortcoming, however, was that he never was quite ready for battle, always seeking more supplies, more reinforcements, and degrading the upper ranks above him. In war it was the stolid and truculent Grant who garnered the power of high command by being himself.

18. *A reputation for fair dealing is a source of power.* People who have high trust from others can persuade them more readily than those whose ability to generate confidence in others is limited. In negotiation the truth and plain speaking, which others can rely upon as being your honest opinion, will carry the day in many cases. Eldridge Cleaver put it, "Doing good is a hustle, too."

Speaking one way in private and another in public can lower your negotiation skills and strengths. If people believe that when you say something is true you actually believe it is true, and when you say you will do something you will actually do it, you have power to arrive at agreement and make them bend to your way in crucial situations.

Now use the following check list to rate your own ability to use power in negotiating.

	Yours	The Other Party's
1. Identify goals. Construct a portfolio of needs and wants.	————	————
2. When does a decision have to be reached?	————	————
3. Who is the key person?	————	————
4. The situation—what exists—the trends.	————	————
5. Five most important specific power factors in this situation (refer to the 18 rules and choose the top 5).	————	————
6. Susceptibility to influence.	————	————

	Yours	The Other Party's
7. What factors can block use of power? How can you avoid them? Meet them?	_____	_____

8. Best strategy and tactics for using power.
  • Means of attaining goals
  • Trading areas
  • Defensive plan
	_____	_____

9. Alternate strategy and tactics. Do you have options?	_____	_____

10. Concentrations.
  • Specific areas for effort
  • Timing
  • Costs
	_____	_____

11. Opportunities for collaboration and mutual gains.	_____	_____
12. Feedback of use of power. To what extent were your goals achieved? Feeling about outcome. What did you learn?	_____	_____

7

Persuasion as a Form of Power

> The most important thing in an argu-
> ment next to being right is to leave
> an escape hatch for your opponent so
> that he can swing over to your side
> gracefully without too much apparent
> loss of face.
> —SYDNEY J. HARRIS

The end of the season had come for the 4H Club and the kids were auctioning off their sheep, which they had raised from lambs. One little girl's sheep was being bid, and she was observed to be crying. The bidding rose higher and higher, and the higher it went the more she cried. A wealthy rancher finally bid $1,000, won the auction, and then turned about and donated the sheep back to the weeping little girl. Several months later the same rancher was a judge in an essay contest for the local school, and one of the submissions was from the same little girl. One crucial passage of her essay described the auction. "The higher they bid for my sheep, the happier I became," she wrote. "I was so happy I was crying. The happier I got, the more I cried. Finally my sheep sold for $1,000, and the man who paid more than I ever dreamed possible, gave my sheep back to me. When I got home my dad barbecued it. It was really delicious." A tear, a word, a gesture may be more persuasive than millions of dollars, armies, or muscle.

While there are those who hold tightly to the opinion that only money talks, experienced negotiators know that money isn't the only thing that talks. A manufacturer's representative once told us, "All of the words and jabber are just so much witch-doctoring, hooting and yelling. It is *price alone* that throws the spear, that kills the other side." He was not, his company reported, a very successful salesman or negotiator. He didn't realize the power which lies in persuasion.

People of action and wealth often don't realize the power of persuasion, even when they are being persuaded. Many of the qualities and skills which make a fine commander, manager, or dynamic leader are useless in the specialized field of verbal combat where words, logic, information, and wit are the weapons which must be worked. Power is a continuum which has at one end the rewards and punishments held by a party to negotiations and at the other end the persuasive powers (see Fig. 7-1). Few people can devote full time to both, and therefore it is frequently found that the best negotiator is not the owner or final decision maker. Famous trial lawyers have often been faced with seemingly open-and-shut cases against their clients, but have through the power of persuasion turned the case around and their client was not only acquitted but in some cases ended up as folk heroes. While we will examine specific tactics of the skilled negotiator in practice in a subsequent chapter, in this one we look at persuasion as a dimension of the previous chapter—as a form of power.

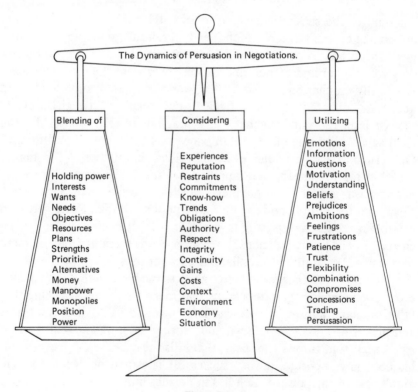

The Dynamics of Persuasion in Negotiations.

Blending of	Considering	Utilizing
Holding power	Experiences	Emotions
Interests	Reputation	Information
Wants	Restraints	Questions
Needs	Commitments	Motivation
Objectives	Know-how	Understanding
Resources	Trends	Beliefs
Plans	Obligations	Prejudices
Strengths	Authority	Ambitions
Priorities	Respect	Feelings
Alternatives	Integrity	Frustrations
Money	Continuity	Patience
Manpower	Gains	Trust
Monopolies	Costs	Flexibility
Position	Context	Combination
Power	Environment	Compromises
	Economy	Concessions
	Situation	Trading
		Persuasion

Figure 7-1.

Figure 7-2.

WHAT IS PERSUASION POWER?

Persuasion means getting other people to do things we want them to do—often by making them believe that the revised act is of their own choosing. Persuasion is based upon four elements, as seen in Fig. 7-2.

1. *Control Over Resources*. Being a millionaire creates considerable influence for the holder of such wealth, who frequently finds that paths are smoothed and obstacles overcome simply because people know of his wealth. Fund raisers know that the best person to chair a fund-raising drive for a university or for United Way is often the wealthiest member of the community. Not that they will personally donate enough to push the campaign over the top, but rather that they will have considerable persuasion power when they send letters or call on others to make a donation.

Personal ownership of resources isn't always necessary. Having effective control over them is just as good. The president of United States Steel or IBM has, at least in title, the control of countless billions of dollars and the support of thousands and thousands of empoyees under his command. We see in the owner or controller of resources the power to do any of the following if he or she were to so decide:

- They might offer us rewards for going along with them.
- They might deny us rewards which we clearly hope to get as a result of a favorable decision on their part.
- They might exact penalties upon us by creating obstacles.

- They might remove obstacles which stop us from getting where we want to go, and do it easily and effortlessly, where we ourselves are blocked without hope of success from overcoming them.
- Their aura of power will swing reluctant people in the desired direction, even if they humbly disavow any intent to throw their weight around.
- Since they have money and the power that goes with it, they are more likely to associate with similar people of equal power, and they have more influence than you or I in getting their cooperation and support.

Great resources either owned or controlled have considerable power of persuasion even when there is no intent to actually throw them into the bargaining situation.

People who write to large organizations often address their pleas to the president, who will perhaps never read the petition but will refer it to a lesser functionary. This does not defeat the writer's purpose, for it might be interpreted by the lesser ranks as a kind of evidence that the top man actually does have a personal bias in favor of the request, or has a personal connection with the writer. A penciled notation on the letter to an aide to "please handle this" will at least assure the writer a reply, and probably a polite one, even when it is negative.

Cunning people often use this power of persuasion to their advantage by alluding to resources they control or own, even when the resources are nonexistent. A clever insurance man named Jones rented an office right over a bank, and carefully placed his desk and chair right over the main vault where the bank's millions were stored. He then hired a sign painter to prepare the following sign:

SAM JONES INSURANCE, My assets over ten million dollars.

Whether or not Sam ever made out well in the business, his sign was clear evidence that he understood the persuasive power of resources and their control in negotiation.

2. *Personality and Behavioral Skills.* The persuader has some skills which others often lack. Psychologists have studied various occupational personalities for decades. While they have not been especially successful in identifying a common set of personality traits for the persuader, it is recognized that there are certain kinds of people who have an apparent

ability to get their way where others are turned back time and time again. Michael Maccoby has identified the modern manager who moves fastest as the "Gamesman," which suggests that persuasion over the long haul tends to be treated as a game by those people who do best at persuading others to promote them, give them bigger responsibilities, and hand them stewardship of great organizations. Eugene Jennings, a management scholar, suggests that being "maze bright"—the ability to negotiate a maze—is a skill of people who rise in organizations. Raw intelligence as measured by testing, on the other hand, is useful in building negotiation power only when it is of a special sort. High IQ, that of the scientist, mathematician, or engineer, is not a requirement. Rather it is the ability to see new and unique combinations from existing facts and to find novel and original solutions to deadlocked positions. The ability to hold a vast amount of information in mind, and to relate the various elements to one another for unique purposes, is one such skill. Often this creates the impression of new intelligence to the other side, and has a distinct kind of persuasive power.

William Buckley, the conservative editor and TV personality, is widely admired, even by such opponents as John K. Galbraith, for his mastery of the language and an ability to state propositions which are detested by the other side with grace and fluidity. Similarly, Galbraith, a confirmed liberal, is avidly read by his opposition because his grasp of syntax and style are lucid and create the impression of high intelligence. Few businessmen would relish the prospect of debating either on any topic, and to suggest that they would defeat them in persuasive argument because they are richer or command more resources would hardly ease the anxiety they would feel at the prospect.

Ability to relate to a wide range of people and situations is also found among skilled persuaders. Talking with kings and princes and with common laborers in their own terms calls for interactive skills which are formidable tools of persuasion. Being seen as tough and macho by men, and sensitive and warm by women; wise by scholars, and compassionate by the disadvantaged are all results of interactive skills of persuaders.

This skill has been identified by Harvard's B. F. Skinner as "discriminatory behavior." That is, you know that it is proper to sing hymns in church and bawdy songs at a smoker, and never be mixed up between the two. Discrimination, then, means knowing when to talk and when to shut up, when to be angry and when to be pleasing and ingratiating, when to dominate and when to submit. There is a time to flatter and a time to deride, to take command and to display obeisance. The discriminating person is often a product of a rather intensive kind of education, in manners, in style, in speech and conduct. The prep school, the Ivy League university, and the graduate school of law and public service often state that the training of their graduates in such conduct is their objective. In a few of their graduates this actually occurs.

How to acquire such discriminating powers as a personal repertory is difficult to prescribe. For some it never comes. Rich kids flunk out of the finest finishing schools, while youngsters reared in the ghetto may emerge with grace and charm which wins others to them. We know, however, the following things about teaching such a repertory of behavior.

a. It is best started young. This is called *imprinting* when it occurs to the very young. They often have *models* who exhibit the qualities which they later display so easily.

b. It can be assisted by specific training in language, manners, and behavior.

c. Prior experience is a most important influence in producing such persuasive ability through discrimination. Modeling of older examples is crucial, as is the social and cultural environment in which one is reared. Lawyers' kids are most apt to be pressed into debate teams, and teachers' children have more respect for learning. While there are exceptions, the rule is worthy of generalizing.

All of this is fine, if you happend to have the wisdom to have been born into the right family, or raised in the right neighborhood, or went to the right prep school. But suppose you didn't? Does this mean you can never improve your personal behavioral skills to improve your negotiation ability? Of course you can. There are some very specific courses you can take, and practices you can engage in which will sharpen your negotiating abilities and your persuasion power.

a. *You can improve your presentation skills.* Courses in presentation methods, public speaking, debating, and argumentation will all make you a better persuader. Such courses are commonplace in evening adult education programs, and have a good track record in changing people's behavior for the better. If you are fumbling, hesitant, or nervous in presentations and discussion, either go learn how to operate in that milieu or stay out of negotiations in an active role.

b. *Language skills* will help your persuasion power. Start with vocabulary, and add to your inventory of useful words which you can bring to bear. Then study and practice your sentence construction abilities and develop more artful ways of saying things for maximum impact. Finally you can learn to develop arguments in paragraphs and entire brief essays to maximize their impact. All of which you can study, practice, and improve upon.

c. *Argumentation and debate* are the essence of the personal skills of persuasion, and if you aren't on top of the key principles here, go take a course, enroll in a Toastmasters' Club, take a Dale Carnegie course, or ask your company training department to bring in an instructor to coach you in debate, bargaining, and negotiation.

3. *Information as a Force in Persuasion.* Persuasion should be aimed at changing behavior of the other side, getting them to quit doing what they have been doing, or doing something new which they haven't been doing. It is pretty simple to overlook how powerful pure raw *information,* unvarnished and free of generalizations and conclusions, can be in persuading others.

A large retail chain in the Midwest was in the midst of a great sales drive to persuade customers to sign up for credit cards. All of their clerical and sales people were given a sales training course on credit cards— how they would benefit the customer, how to sell, how to overcome arguments, and how to prompt people to complete the application. However, the course didn't really go into details on how the form should be filled out. As a result, hundreds of applications were completed with incomplete information, since the form was rather complex and easy to botch up. Over in the office where credit was checked, the information had never arrived that a large sales campaign for credit cards was under way, and suddenly a flood of credit applications began to pour in. The overworked credit investigators were dismayed at the sudden heavy work load, and protested to their boss that they couldn't keep up.

"Just do the best you can, and stick with the manual for handling applications," she told her people. Accordingly they made many credit judgments based upon incomplete or wrongly completed applications. This meant that many people were turned down because they hadn't filled in the blanks properly, creating a terrible customer relations problem. People who had been given a heavy sales pitch subsequently received a curt form letter telling them that their credit wasn't good enough and they were denied a credit card. This made them furious at the company and they not only didn't buy on credit, but further, stopped shopping in that store for cash as well. One day the vice president for merchandising happened to run across a report from the credit department on the ratio of people who had been rejected for credit. Thinking it to be exceptionally high, he went to the credit department and talked to the credit manager, demanding that she be a little more lenient about credit. "If you people are going to be so picky we will never have any customers," he complained. The credit manager was offended by this smirch upon her professional performance and responded hotly that they were following all of the rules in applying credit standards. The negotiations ended without a satisfactory resolution of the problem. The sales people continued to push for credit cards applications, and the credit department continued to reject many of them for clerical errors on the forms.

It was only because a systems consultant happened to run across the situation that it was resolved. What the consultant provided was new information to the two parties: (1) that the applications weren't being filled out properly, and (2) that the people selling the credit cards had no idea that their efforts were being thwarted by this bad application form. Once the information was presented to the two sides, the vice president for merchandising and the credit manager got together and worked out a satisfactory solution. They quickly redesigned the credit application form, conducted a brief but clear training session for all clerks, and then provided weekly feedback to the sales people as to which of the applications they submitted had been accepted for credit cards and which had been rejected, and the reasons for it. The number of rejections dropped sharply. The original negotiations had been based solely upon the use of authority. "I demand that you ease your picky standards" had been opposed by "I am credit manager and have the authority to decide who shall be approved." Since each had independent authority, it was a deadlock of traditional power negotiation. It was the introduction of new information into the proceeding which caused them to arrive at a mutually satisfactory conclusion.

Information should have these characteristics:

a. It should be accurate, factual, and based upon evidence.
b. It should be specialized and explicit, not general.
c. It should be timely, for there is nothing more useless than information which is too late.
d. It should be situational, that is, it should be related to the problems, the people, where the resources are, and who controls it.

e. It should relate to the organizational status of the people sending and receiving it.

f. It should be based upon a need to know and the authority of people sending and receiving. The vice president's headache may be more important than that of the stock boy.

4. *Strategies Exercised Produce Persuasion Power.* A desk officer in the U.S. Department of State is a trained diplomatic officer whose function is to monitor all of the incoming messages, information, and reports from a particular nation and to prepare informed and useful situation reports for the bureau chief in an area of the world such as Europe, East Asia, and so forth. The chief of the Latin American bureau one year found that several of his desk officers were not anticipating significant changes in a couple of important Latin American nations. While their reports on economics, politics, military, and similar categories were factual and contained all of the information which was available, nonetheless it seemed that they weren't seeing soon enough many of the changes in government policy which were being produced. Often the legislature in Aspirinia, a Central American republic, was passing legislation which was contrary to American interests, and the bureau chief and Secretary of State weren't learning about the possibility of such moves until after the acts had been accomplished. It became apparent to the bureau chief that raw information wasn't enough, but rather should be supplemented with a strategy which would help anticipate such legislation. After one especially embarrassing incident, he met with his desk officers and they developed a strategy for monitoring legislative actions in the desk officers' respective countries. It was as follows:

The embassy in each country was given a four-step rating system for their reporting of impending legislation. Each level produced some rating points for the embassy involved and the desk officer handling that nation's affairs. The desk officer and ambassador would receive a score of zero if a piece of legislation affecting American interests was discovered only after it had been enacted into law. This was the lowest score and would be considered a failure. The next step was rated as one-point performance: The embassy and desk officer would report that legislature was being considered for introduction and the American position had been stated to the subject nation. The next highest level scored three points if the desk officer and ambassador not only knew about the proposed law, and had stated their case, but further had succeeded in persuading the other nation to amend or eliminate unfavorable legislation. At the fourth level a rating of four points was given when the ambassador and desk officer had sufficient advance information about the proposed legislation so that Washington was able to formulate a policy statement on the proposed law. In this category, it was often possible for the embassy to actually assist in the shaping of the law, in some cases even producing the desired wording. All of this of course would be done without any complaints about interference by the United States in the internal affairs of the subject nation, in which case the whole score would revert back to zero.

The desk officers, having helped shape the strategy, knew how it should work, and kept their own scores in managing the American interest in the target nations thereafter.

Simply having data, statistics, and current opinions and trends wasn't enough. Such was what statisticians call a "necessary but not sufficient condition." Rather, a guiding strategic plan was required for coping with the entire situation in the light of the realities of the nation and its importance to us.

Luck, it should be noted, is an element in making strategy work, but as one eminent sports manager noted, "Luck is the product of preparation meeting opportunity."

NINETEEN KEYS TO PERSUASION

In order to get people to do what you want them to do, you might consider the following nineteen keys and *rate yourself* on each on a scale of 1 to 5.

1. Persuade yourself. Do you have confidence in your case and have you a high enough expectation level? _____

2. How good are your track record, reputation, and credentials with the other side? _____

3. Have you chosen the right time and place and prepared the meeting place carefully to help your case? _____

4. Do you have an attention-getting lead into the situation, such as an opening offer that will be attractive to the other side?   _____

5. Can you start with areas where agreement can be reached most easily?   _____

6. Do you know what will arouse wants and needs in the other side?   _____

7. Do you try to stress the desirability of agreement and what will create interest in producing a change in the other side?   _____

8. Do you know how to listen fully before making judgments and rebuttals?   _____

9. How will you handle objections? Are you prepared to meet them before they arise?   _____

10. Can you restate the other side's position as clearly as they themselves could state it?   _____

11. Are you ready with a specific proposal: what, where, when, how, and why?   _____

12. What time limits should you set, and upon what items?   _____

13. Can you find common ground and similarities in the two positions, yours and theirs?   _____

14. Do you have a system for tracking your progress toward your goals?   _____

15. Are you using the power of repetition and persistence, turning the other person's arguments into an occasion for restating common goals and your position?   _____

16. Are you avoiding placing the other side on the defensive, thus arousing emotional responses which will block progress to their change?   _____

17. Do you have an explicit conclusion in mind, and are you ready to settle fast when you reach it?   _____

18. Do you concentrate upon the features and benefits of your case first, leaving money price and terms of payment to the end?   _____

19. Are you willing to be fooled just a little bit, and
to avoid overkilling the other side to produce
mutual gain?   _____

                            Total Points   _____

A perfect score would be 95 points. If you rate 90 or over, you are probably going to do a great
job of persuasion.

80 points means you have a superior chance.

70 points means you should restudy your strategy, tactics, and information again to heighten
your chances of producing change.

Under 60 points: postpone the meeting and do some more homework.

RESISTING PERSUASION BY OTHERS

In a large management association the boss was a prestigious man, with
immense power of persuasion. One of the division managers reported
the following: "I would get a call from Larry to come to his office, and
I often knew exactly what he was going to ask me to do. I would walk
into his office ready to fight, but every time when I walked out I not
only had bought the new assignment or change, but often I was con-
gratulating myself on being such a lucky guy to have this great
opportunity."

In bargaining it helps to have a specific strategic set of rules for resisting the blandishments and cajolery, or the muscle, of the other side. If,
you know that you really don't need or want what the other person is
about to lay upon you, you may produce a better result. Here are some
guides which successful negotiators have used to resist persuasion:

- *Be prepared* with facts, figures, information, and opinions of others
  to counter those which are thrown against you.
- *Set your limits* before you start, and under no circumstance lower
  or raise them immediately without a chance to reflect, caucus, con-
  sult, or sleep on proposals to alter those limits.
- *Use the missing person* as an argument for being unable to make
  changes. "I have to talk this over with my board" or perhaps a boss
  or other permitter in the background will help slow down the rush
  of their persuasion.

- *Have alternatives ready* for their proposals, and anticipate when and in what form theirs will show up in negotiation. When they propose a reasonable course, be quick to accept it if you have had such an option in mind. That acceptance is to your benefit and the other side's both.
- *Plead poverty.* You can agree in principle but then tell them that you can't accept because of budgetary limits or unavailability of resources, people, or space to go along with their idea. This opens the road to a revision closer to your needs and wants.
- *Monopolize the discussion.* Occasionally a filibuster is indicated in which you keep talking, interjecting lengthy background statements, historical background, and complicating factors until you wear them out. This will buy time if nothing else.
- *Change the subject.* When the other person introduces a sensitive and critical point which you sense is your weakness, change the subject abruptly. One good technique when another places some vital and damaging evidence on a chart pad or blackboard is to quickly rise and erase it before it becomes fixed in everyone's mind and write something else on the board, filling the space with a new topic.
- *Silence is golden.* If the other side introduces a telling point which they don't immediately recognize as that important, don't heighten it by panicky rebuttals and defensive and angry replies. Rather, remain silent on it, stand up and stretch, have a side conversation, go for a break, yawn, but don't answer it.
- *Call a recess.* If you get the feeling you are being stampeded or have just lost a crucial point in debate, feign fatigue, or the need for a rest, and suggest an early lunch, an early adjournment for the day. When you come back, pick up on an entirely new subject.
- *Postpone decisions* before you deadlock fully. Suggest "Let's drop this item for a while and come back to it later. What I'd like to bring up are some details of that proposal we were talking about two days ago."
- *Say no decisively.* Learn the value of saying no, "hell no," "no way," "absolutely not," "never," and the like. This may be a firm expression of your limit, or it may be a technique for softening their original demand and producing some alternative proposal which moves things a little in your direction. Don't be coy about saying no.

- *Walk away.* On occasion you may have to simply fold up your papers and walk out. If the other side is being sticky about an unreasonable and unthinkable position, explain to them that you see it that way, and threaten to walk. If they resist, you may find it sensible to actually walk. "We'll see you in court," etc.

8
Winning Tactics—Aggressiveness in Negotiation

> The president has the power to
> make deals, answer questions,
> provide assurances, funnel
> information, ease doubts and
> massage egos . . .
> —STEVEN V. ROBERTS

On October 28, 1981, a hard-fought month of negotiations led person-ally by President Ronald Reagan resulted in a favorable vote in the Senate permitting the sale of Awacs plane and other air combat equip-ment to Saudi Arabia. The action gave the President and his adminis-tration an important legislative victory when only days before he had faced the prospect of defeat by a wide vote margin. The following morn-ing's papers showed a beaming Reagan displaying a roll call roster of those who had voted on each side of the issue. Appearing fresh and energetic after the battle, the President obviously enjoyed winning over his opponents in a protracted process of negotiation which had started out with seeming defeat, turned about by his own personal negotiating skills. Even his political foes conceded that it was "an awesome dis-play." Chagrined foes of the measure were forced to concede that they had been bested by a zesty and masterful display of persuasion and negotiation. All of the forces of promise, aura, information persuasion, and even some threats to withhold funds for local projects had been thrown into this all-out battle of words. The President had demon-strated not only the powers of his office, but considerable relish for this kind of negotiation.

LEARNING TO ENJOY NEGOTIATION—THE FIRST STEP

People who do well in the heat of battle over conflicting interests, wants, and needs almost inevitably enjoy the process. Some observers were quick to contrast the effectiveness of President Reagan with the obvious lack of it on the part of his predecessor, Jimmy Carter. Carter, it was noted, was reluctant to enter such energetic and spirited give-and-take with Congress. More private in personality, Carter was apparently less enthused about doing battle with his political foes, or even members of his own party. He often failed to line up his own allies fully, stated conclusions without taking time to provide backup and support information, dealt less fully with questions, and was most reluctant to engage in the white lies which massage egos and win opponents to his side.

WHY WE ENJOY NEGOTIATION

Surveys of executives attending executive development programs, found twelve major reasons we learn to enjoy negotiating:

- We realize it is a way of getting what we need and want. The importance, urgency, or even nobility of the end result is the major reasons we learn to like bargaining. Those for whom it has worked have learned to enjoy the process as well as the end result.
- We see it as an essential method of doing business.
- The prospect of winning and the probability of doing so cause us to enter the process with pleasurable anticipation. Such anticipation generates more than enough energy to do all of the myriad things needed to win. Without such energy and zest we do a bad job in handling the numerous details required, and we lose.
- Negotiation is exciting. The urgency of momentary crises, the rising of immediate small goals, and the challenge of solving difficult problems and overcoming high barriers makes it stimulating for both sides. This gamelike characteristic is attractive to important people.
- To enter negotiation and win produces a sensation of being alert, wise, and quick of wit, all of which are favorable sensations. A high sense of self-esteem can follow victory, or even a worthy defeat.
- We come away from the experience with the feeling that we have learned, grown, matured, and mastered our situation despite its complexity. This sense of mastery is a strong motive for action.
- It is the "thing to do," for the respect of society is often accorded the skilled negotiator, the socially adept person, or the leader who can sway other opinions to his or her own.

- We develop skills in negotiation which we are pleased to have acquired. The lawyer or bargainer who must master vast amounts of information and organize it for effective persuasion senses that personal growth has taken place, which produces favorable self-perception and self-liking.
- The thrill of victory matched by the agony of defeat are important ego-building elements in negotiation. A basic need, suggests psychologist Abraham Maslow, is that of ego building, and negotiation can offer such nourishment of ego strength.
- Team effort is very likely to be involved in major negotiations, and the sense of gregariousness, belonging, and camaraderie which is also a basic motivator is fed and increased.
- Negotiation is a vehicle for displaying power and indicates a compelling characteristic to the winner. Power is the one satisfier of human wants which apparently is inexhaustible and insatiable.
- Negotiation is a diversion from the ordinary, the routine, the boring. Each negotiation is a feeder for our appetite for crises. We enjoy the emergencies which we complain about, and seek out the social problem, the special opportunity which negotiation provides.

WHY WE HESITATE TO NEGOTIATE

The same people who responded with their reasons for enjoying negotiation as a process also gave reasons why they sometime hesitate to negotiate. Fourteen reasons were often stated by these informants:

- They lack confidence in their own abilities in negotiation to win what they need and want. Many bosses prefer to be directive rather than go through the negotiation involved in Management by Objectives. Some people who have ample resources prefer to pay the first or asking price rather than try and fail in bargaining with a zealous bargainer.
- Fear of consequences was stated as the second reason for hesitating to plunge into bargaining situations. The possibility of failure and subsequent embarrassment, or the possibility of offending the other party by being too assertive, produces caution and timidity in negotiation and probable failure. Traditionally, women have not been seen as hard bargainers in such transactions as asking for greater opportunity for promotion, or higher pay, in part because such self-

assertion did not suit the traditional feminine image. Of late, however, assertiveness training and successful experience have reduced this fear in many modern women managers.

- Fear of losing makes us hesitate to negotiate. The dread of plunging boldly onward to an obvious defeat is natural.
- The great amount of time consumed by negotiations was another reason that many people cited to explain their distaste for it. Victory often goes to the side which throws in the longest hours, the greatest expenditure of energy, and the ready use of overtime, weekends, and holidays to prepare and execute. Negotiation is quite unlike regular responsibility. The labor negotiator who travels constantly, lives out of a suitcase, stays at hotels of mixed quality, and misses regular meals is a rule rather than an exception. Such a life style is not for everyone.
- The patience required to negotiate is a negative for many action-centered executives. They would prefer to bark the crisp order, direct things to happen, and not have to bother with listening and adapting. Having the patience to hear the same story told for the thirtieth time and to engage in the same pointless disputes run over again and again may be perfectly sensible stragegy for the negotiator, but it turns some off. Without patience you won't enjoy negotiating.
- Fear of the unknown bars others from enjoying negotiation. They haven't done it, can't imagine what it is like, and thus have some apprehension about its effect upon them.
- It is hard, grueling work. Not only the long hours, but the need for constant attention, concentration, and steady interchange with people who disagree with you is physically and emotionally draining on some.
- It requires extensive preparation and a planned strategy, which is unappealing to many who would rather work in an environment where winging it and shooting from the hip is more acceptable.
- Negotiations are likely to arouse emotional fervor at some time, and this in itself turns some managers off. They prefer to conduct their entire managerial life without displays of emotion. Fear, anger, and the like impose a tax on the person using them, and the good negotiator often employs them as part of his bargaining tactics.

- Some people avoid negotiations because they are afraid to say no. They feel that being negative will cause other people to dislike them, a condition which they are unprepared to provoke. If you can't say "no," then negotiation is not your cup of tea.
- Others hesitate to negotiate because they view the entire process as evidence of poverty or penuriousness and they wish to be seen as monied, upper-class, generous, and wealthy. These are the conspicuous consumers for whom haggling over a price would be utterly foreign, and accordingly most negotiations are offensive, welcomed only by lowbrows.
- Natural procrastinators often find that negotiation is not a suitable method of doing business for them. They would not enjoy the immediacy, the urgency, and the dynamic action which can occur in negotiation. For many managers, nothing is urgent enough to occur immediately. Everything can be "let's plan that for next week" or "better wait until fall on that." Negotiation is frequently inescapably urgent.
- Crooks and people having guilty knowledge of themselves don't like negotiations, for it might expose things they wish with all their heart to conceal. In the give-and-take of bargaining, all sorts of undercover facts may emerge, and crooks have something to hide.
- A sense of powerlessness causes people to avoid negotiation. The idea that "I am too low and too lacking in clout" makes the prospect of entering a tough bargaining environment fearsome and distasteful.

With a high level of enjoyment anticipated, you will plunge into negotiation with the level of enthusiasm and tenacity which will help you succeed. With nothing but a heap of worries and fears casting themselves over you as you enter the process, you will most likely do poorly.

The first step in winning negotiations, the first tactic if you will, is to persuade yourself that it will work, that you have a better than average chance to win, and that you will enjoy the entire process win or lose.

While this has a kind of self-hypnosis suggestion to it, it's nonetheless a fundamental principle, a hard law which you must wrap around yourself or leave the battlefield before you get killed. This is a kind of self-discipline, and if you fail this criteria, don't bother reading any further. Simply hire a lawyer, or engage a more zestful advocate, give them your full confidence, and retire to your closet to await whatever fate your champion can produce. Check the twelve reasons people enjoy, and the fourteen they don't enjoy listed above, and see how they balance out for yourself. If the fourteen dominate the twelve by a wide margin, don't enter the ring. Do as the draftees did in the Civil War: hire a substitute to go in your place. However ignoble and cowardly this may be made to seem by your associates, it can lengthen your life.

HOW TO GET STARTED IN NEGOTIATING—USE PRE-NEGOTIATIONS BARGAINING TO SET THE STAGE

Walking into negotiations cold means that the first few days will be spent defining the issues, finding areas of agreement and disagreement, and sizing up the strengths and weaknesses of the other side. This is a dangerous part of negotiation unless you have set the stage for the sessions in advance. While it isn't always possible to engage in such pre-negotiation dealing, you should make every effort to do so. If you are flying to Manila and have only two days to bargain a whole new arrangement with a distributor there, you won't be able to follow many of the pre-negotiation precepts there. Therefore you should plan to incorporate many of them into the first stages of negotiation, for they set the stage, position your side, and give you a better chance of arriving at mutually agreed upon solutions to your problems.

John Dunlop and Derek Bok in their book *Labor and the American Community* list a number of pre-negotiation techniques which they have observed on the labor negotiations scene. To these we might add several others from commercial and from superior-subordinate (MBO) relationships. They include the following:

1. *Call some informal conferences* in advance of the actual negogiations to set the stage, find the issues, define objectives, and allow people to state their rationale and problems. Used successfully in the apparel industry, this is a semiformal way of opening the bargaining without being under the pressure of contract closing dates or other time pressures.

2. *Jointly finance some special studies* in general areas of mutual interest to both parties. Safety in the plant, the problems of an aging

work force, and practices in industrial engineering would be typical topics.

3. *Start the negotiations well in advance* of the actual deadline date, or the expiration of any old contract. Applied in the meat packing industry, this alleviated strikes, produced a more orderly exploration of all of the issues, and produced more agreement.

4. *Use outside neutral parties* to mediate or provide fact-finding recommendations on some strategic issues and long-standing areas of disagreement. This was used by Kaiser Industries in negotiations with the Steelworkers.

5. *Establish industry wide mediation mechanisms* where individual firms are deadlocked. The rest of the industry and unions throw their influence into producing agreements through impartial mediators acceptable to both parties.

6. *Joint study committees* of the kind used in the steel industry focus upon key issues which are the subject of negotiations—wages, hours, conditions of work, productivity, standards, and the like. Those studies often produce the basis for creative solution to sticky problems in advance.

7. *Economic studies* and ongoing economic investigations to provide factual economic data for both sides, as used in the shoe industry, can eliminate pointless and uninformed argument.

8. *The use of binding arbitration* through prior agreement made before the actual bargaining of a specific contract begins can help. This system is employed in professional baseball, the steel industry, and in some public utility bargaining.

9. *Ordinary arbitration* clauses are included in most contracts to deal with rights, and with selected issues on a case-by-case basis for the arbitration of interests.

In addition to these examples of pre-negotiation relationships in labor-management negotiation, there are others which experienced negotiators report have served well in pre-negotiation actions.

- *Face-to-face contacts* and conversations with individual members of the other side can establish a personal knowledge of the principal figures on the other side. This "softens" each to realize that the other person is a genuine person, with serious interests and a willingness to relate on a reasonable level. Often such contacts are strictly social: dinners, luncheons, fishing trips, and the like.

- *Communication of general information* about your side to the other side as an educational effort aids understanding. Financial reports sent to stockholders can also be sent to unions, suppliers, customers, and employees. New product releases which are available to limited interest groups can be distributed more widely to help produce familiarity with the firm and its products among those who will be in negotiation. Press releases can be distributed more widely than simply to the journals and media in which placement is sought. This gives the other side some sense of being in the know before reading it in the media.

The objective of pre-negotiation tactics is to provide the other side with the equivalent of a long personal acquaintance, thus making agreement satisfactory to both sides more likely.

It is exactly this process of education which heightens the likelihood of an agreement with which both sides can live. Well-orchestrated pre-negotiations tactics should be considered an integral part of the negotiation process.

SETTING THE AGENDA FOR NEGOTIATING SESSIONS

Whether it be labor negotiations, purchasing agreements, merger transactions, or superior-subordinate relations (MBO), there are ten standard items which should appear in the agenda of most negotiations. While no standard checklist of stages is possible or advisable, these ten, our research shows, appear frequently in most negotions.

1. *Developing Common Objectives.* Despite conflicts of interests and goals, there are areas of common benefit and a desire to arrive at agreement. Identifying these common objectives and referring to them throughout the bargaining sessions is essential for both sides.
2. *Areas of Difference.* A progressive step is to decide the subject matters on which there is lack of agreement, the degree of these differences, their relative importance, and priorities.
3. *Using Experiences.* Focusing attention on specific happenings, incidents, problems, and experiences of mutual interest will gain more than discussing abstractions and principles.

4. *Defining Terms.* Misunderstandings often occur over terminology.
5. *Listening.* Try to give attention in order to gain understanding of the other sides positions and to recognize concessions and counteroffers.
6. *Trade-offs.* Give as well as take is part of bargaining. Benefits require pay through trade-offs. Each party leaves the negotiations with some reward rather than a "win-lose."
7. *Narrowing Differences.* Negotiations require the differences between parties to be narrowed progressively.
8. *Keeping Open Position.* Minimize stalemates, ridicule, abuse, boxing into a corner, or break-offs. Showing respect and consideration avoids hardening of a position. Offer alternative methods of achieving a common goal. Blend interests, don't depend too much on logic.
9. *Personalities.* Know yourself, the group you represent, and get to know the persons with whom you negotiate.
10. *Agreement.* Recognize when you are close to agreement—whether by voice, gestures, expression, or lack of objections. Close the deal. Don't overkill or lose the agreement by continued selling. Make sure each party has gained and that the agreement will have mutual benefits.

WINNING TACTICS AND HOW TO USE THEM

Once the negotiation is joined, there is no substitute for hard bargaining. Your reasonableness has already been demonstrated during the pre-negotiation, and your strategies provide you with a game plan. Your personal strategy will determine the best personal demeanor you will adopt and stick with. There are some important elements in the tactics of negotiations which we'll defer to later chapters. These are the defensive aspects: dealing from a weak position, making concessions, and a chapter on managing timing in negotiation. The tactics in this immediate chapter are offensive in nature and comprise your attack plan. While there are several possible outcomes—domination, submission, open war, or strike—the best results will be the arrival at an agreement which is acceptable to both sides. This won't be achieved, however, if you are the only one who is reasonable and generous, for the best agreement will come when each side puts its best foot forward and states its case, advocating its position and principles with every argument and every ounce of energy possible. It is exactly out of this conflict of wills that the limiting conditions of the two sides will emerge, and a mutually acceptable agreement achieved.

USING A GOOD OFFENSE AS THE BEST DEFENSE

The objective in offensive action in negotiation is to establish control in your hands. Unless you make such a campaign early, you may find that their efforts to achieve the same objective will gain that position for them, and you may be forced into a corner where you settle on terms unsatisfactory to you. Plan to be aggressive in a cool and civil manner. Here are some of the guides to aggressive tactics:

1. *Be sure you are dealing with equals or superiors,* never inferiors. Right off the bat, find out what the authority of your counterparts is to make deals. Negotiate only with those who have as much authority as you do. They have a distinct advantage if they have a hidden approver in the background who could upset any agreements they make, unless you have the same kind of organization plan. If you can deal with their top honcho while you have a backup absent third party, you have a leverage over them. In a pinch you can fall back on that absent decider: "I have to check this" is a fine recourse when things get rough, and you might even request your hidden superior to reverse you for tactical purposes. If you have this third party and they don't, you have an advantage. Try to get it.

2. *When on the offensive, don't haggle over numerous small issues.* Start with the vital first. If you can control the agenda, you have some control over what can be said, and when it will be introduced. The order in which topics arise can work to your advantage, and you should stick in your heels over the shape of the agenda. If they get tough on this one, make the subject of choosing the agenda one of the items which is to be deferred.

3. *Temper hard-nose with apparent friendliness.* If things get too formal, take time to introduce everyone around the table if they haven't already been introduced. Interject personal comments of a friendly and perhaps jovial nature, produce a laugh, and even throw out a few self-deprecating remarks, without creating any doubt that you are a *serious person.*

4. *Try to fix the burden of proof on the other side.* This is a variant of the question "Who is the customer here?" and it isn't always determined by the facts of the situation. A buyer may not hold the trump cards if the supplier has a product in short supply. In such a case, it is the buyer who must do the selling and the burden of proof lies there. In mergers, it is the target firm which may have the strength, and the pursuer the burden of proof. If you can shift the burden of proof to the other side, they they become the petitioner and you the judge and decider.

In a large veterans' hospital, there were plenty of pharmacists, but a crucial shortage of pathologists. The director of the hospital, who often conducted the hiring negotiations with senior staff applicants, told us, "I tell the pharmacists exactly what the hours and pay will be, and inform them that we expect promptness. With the pathologists, however, I often ask, 'What hours would you like to work, Doctor?' " The crucial employee often has more latitude in defining his job, where the easily replaced worker must accept what is offered. Knowing the other side's vulnerabilities will help you shift the burden of proof, and you should take care of this firmly, very early in negotiation.

5. *Always make your first demand stiff* and higher than you ultimately expect to settle for. Chester Karass, the negotiations expert, reports that in his study of over 2,000 executives high demands pay off in better end results. Buyers should make low initial offers, sellers do better when they make high demands, and unexpectedly high demands produce high results if you are persistent. Unions always go in with a large number of demands, for it gives some chips to be traded away. Avoid being ridiculous, however.

6. *Invariably keep calm and collected,* but get the other side to lose their cool. A manual issued to bargainers for a national electrical union instructs its negotiators to "always play on making the other side angry when things get stuck." They will lose their poise, and in shaking up the situation you may increase the likelihood of their making a major mistake. The danger here is that emotional discharges tend to be contagious. If you make them angry, the sight of an angry person, or the things that are said in anger, may make you angry. This is the time to get a firm grip on yourself and avoid angry responses.

7. *Keep good notes on what has happened.* When the other side has conceded a point, be sure you have a note of the form, wording, and

time of the concession. Be careful of your wording, and don't presume that an item is ready to be signed simply because you have an agreement "in principle." This is actually an understanding or AIP (Agreement in Principle) for which specific wording must be debated. Make notes of changes in demands or offers, and keep records of your own demands and concessions. Type them up daily and distribute them, rather than waiting until the end.

8. *Play the game of Glossary.* During the negotiations never assume that you are using a word with the same meaning that the other side is using it. Similarly, ask them to define their terms. "You talk about the 'night shift.' Do you mean the second shift or the third shift?"

9. *Every time they offer you a morsel, ask for a barrel in trade.* If you have done your strategic planning well, you have a pretty fair idea of what their musts and wants are. When they ask for something you know to be a want but not crucial, ask for one of your own needs in return.

10. *Go to the table loaded with information.* During World War II one of the authors was on the Army side of some negotiations in the Philippines in which two competing groups were petitioning the staff of the Supreme Commander for transport for its divisions. Another Army Corps insisted that it should have top priority, and the rhetoric flowed rather freely. At one point an admiral on the headquarters staff threw out the question, "Exactly what do each of you require by way of shipping, and what will you use it for?" The other side entered a lengthy tirade to establish how its mission was the most important, that its record in combat should entitle it to the kind of logistical support it needed, and that its general was getting pretty damned tired of red tape and bureaucrats in high places stopping him and his boys from winning the war for lack of a few rotten ships, and by God he should not be treated this way, and so on. Our side, during this tirade, referred to a large black notebook which had been brought to the meeting by one of the authors, a minor officer who was part of the team.

"Admiral, we have 1,425 vehicles and 500 trailers that need transport. That will require seven liberty ships now all lying at anchor in Hollandia. They should be at Morotai in four days. Load our equipment and have it in Manila in six days, and we will be out of your hair." Impressed by our hard facts, not only about his own needs, but our knowledge of the location, number, and even the names of the ships, he quickly made his decision in favor of the better-informed. No sooner had he agreed than our winning commander reached into his briefcase and pulled out copies of fully completed orders, including all of the necessary naval paperwork to set the ships in motion within the hour.

Information is a powerful persuader, and when you have it and the other side doesn't, you can assume the offensive and attack with heavy argument. There is a magic quality about facts in business and administrative thinking. The person who has more of them at the right time has a sharp advantage over the person who doesn't. This is where research and investigative digging in advance of negotiation pays off. Knowing what laws apply, what the alternative costs will be, how each alternative will look when turned into money, and what people are involved and what their attitudes are can all be great tools of aggressive negotiation.

In one automobile company a strong argument was going on about alternative models for a couple of years hence. The advocates from the large-car division asserted stoutly that "the customers want comfort style and roadability in cars." The other side, representing smaller models, didn't engage in abstract debate or shouting matches. They quickly produced a hitherto unknown study by a prestigious national sampling organization showing the overpowering desire of customers for smaller, lighter, and more gas-efficient cars. Their survey data won the day.

11. *Use some of the proven tactics of formal debate* to win arguments. One large firm uses a professor of rhetoric who is also a debate coach to brief their important upcoming bargaining session. Such debaters' rules as making sure that the affirmative side is presented first is often violated in negotiation. If the negative side is presented first, then the affirmative may never get a chance to get on the table, for you will be responding to the negatives, which is quite different from presenting the positive position. Make your case as fully and completely as possible before you let the negative side get in its erroneous poison. Further, if you can anticipate what the negative viewpoint might be, try to answer it by rebutting the other side's negative argument before it is ever presented. This robs the other side of the benefit of that argument, for they cannot present it with equal force if it has already been brought up and destroyed by the affirmative. This means that you should try to land on your feet on the affirmative side of the negotiation, even if it is your purpose to do something which might be construed as negative.

12. *Use the tools of logic* to persuade the other side. In addition to

being soundly grounded in facts, the way in which you organize them can swing things your way. The major tools of argument which you can rely on include most of the following:

Use analogies to make your point. An analogy is something which is *like something else.* You can thus show how the other side's proposal is like something which is foolish. "You are throwing out the baby with the bath water" is a common analogy. You can use a single example as an analogy: "Your proposal reminds me of the old woodchopper whose production was going down. When somebody asked him if he had sharpened his axe recently, he replied, 'Nope, I've been too busy chopping wood.'" Even if the example isn't close to the real case, it often persuades. Using physical analogies is often persuasive: "That resembles the Titanic, and you know what happened to that ship." Representational analogy uses colorful phrases such as "Why don't we run our idea up the flagpole and see if anybody salutes it?" Sports analogies like hitting the ball, running for daylight, sending in the plays, and hit and run are analogies which sometimes persuade.

Make appeals to authority: "A move like that probably wouldn't be legal," for example. *Using better numbers* is still another form of argument: "Our studies show that forty percent of the people are strongly opposed to such a pattern," for instance. Use arguments which have been *previously printed* by citing an article you have clipped from a journal. This adds authority to your words. *The weight of dollars* is another variety of appeal to authority: "After all, we have spent twenty million dollars and five years of research on this subject which we think should be weighed heavily in the decision."

The weight of paper which is presented in evidence is still further appeal to authority: "This computer printout denies the entire truth of your position," at which point you hoist seven pounds of printouts onto the table. It is most unlikely that they will read it, and they will have to try something less substantial to offset if. *Arguments to the crowd* may help you line up some authority on your side: "The boys in the shop (or your dealers, or your suppliers) won't like what you will be doing to them, Jim" is such an appeal. *Arguments to times gone or times coming* can add authority to your case as well: "We have been working with your firm for forty years and we think that deserves some consideration"; or, appealing ahead: "As you know, inflation erodes values and we can expect that our suggestion will help inflation-proof your business for several years." *The argument of novelty* is found when we throw some dazzling bit of scientific data into the fray: "Our computer studies based upon later technology and biogenetics shows clearly" has a kind of magic-show appeal about it, especially if you can have an authority of undisputed credentials make such a pitch.

Less satisfactory arguments can be employed, but usually aren't as persuasive and shouldn't be employed loosely, for you are apt to be more vulnerable. Such arguments as *attacking the other side* personally can have adverse long-term affects. This should be used only when your case is so weak as to be hopeless. *Appeals to the emotions* sometimes work, but are likewise risky with experienced opponents. *Appealing to grad-ualism* is a sound technique for delay which can be temporarily hlpful: "Let's put that off until next year." (Check your logical skill in Fig. 8-1.)

	Rate Your Readiness	Points up to 10
1. *Analogies* ("like something else")	—	10
2. *Appeals to authority:*		
Use better numbers	—	5
Printed materials	—	5
Weight of dollars	—	5
Paper documentation	—	5
Appeal to crowd	—	5
Times-past appeal	—	5
Times-coming appeal	—	5
Show novelty	—	5
Total Pluses	==	
		50
3. *Deduct if you have to use these:*		
Personal attacks	—	−10
Emotional appeals	—	− 5
Appeal to gradualism	—	− 1
Total Negatives	==	−16
Grand Total	==	==

Key: 40–50 = Superior; 30–40 = Fair; Under 30 = Poor

Figure 8-1. Check Your Logical Armament in Negotiation.

TAKE CHARGE—BE A LEADER

Less rational in contrast, but more effective in assuming a wining stance, is your ability to provide leadership in the negotiations. This means that you will take charge of things, be a leader, and decide rather than drift as negotiations progress. This doesn't mean you must *dominate* the other side, but rather that you make certain that things are progressing in a responsible fashion toward a mutually satisfactory conclusion. Most people who fail in negotiation do so because they didn't take charge of their own side's case, and of the proposals presented by others. Don't be a puppet in the bargaining, but a fully functioning person. Being an authentic person, not a cunning, clever, and devious one, could be the first rule of assuming this posture. Reading the many books, or attending the many seminars on negotiations available, might arm you with tricks and ruses which will outwit and cause the other person to feel that they have been defeated and may win you a temporary advantage, but may produce long-term loss.

Don't surrender at any stage of the negotiation should be your governing tactic. That's not the same as saying "don't retreat," which of course can be both sensible and beneficial at times. It means that you don't cave in to intimidation, never get swept away by frenzy or passion on their side or yours, don't let frustration erode your patience, and are always ready to face facts with facts of your own. Keep your aches and pains and fatigue from blurring your objective; keep the goal in mind at all times. Make choices constantly as you go, and don't vacillate and waffle over problems and contradictions, but decide.

Be a leader especially in creating ideas on the spot. When deadlock seems endless, that's the time when leadership in creative new ideas is called for. Here in this leadership attitude lies the true key to winning tactics in negotiation.

9
Tactics for Dealing with Equals or Betters

> Life does not consist of holding good cards
> but of playing a poor hand well.
> —THOMAS FULLER

One night a late-arriving husband in his cups trailed into the house followed by a 600-pound gorilla. "This is Harry, our new household pet," he announced to his shocked spouse. Stunned, she could hardly speak. "But where does a 600-pound gorilla sleep?" she asked for lack of anything else to say. Turning to view his giant companion, the husband opined, "Anywhere he wants."

If you are a 600-pound gorilla in negotiations, you can make just about any kind of deal you choose if you wish to get tough about it. But more often than not, the very reason you are considering negotiation is that you aren't the 600-pounder, or even the 100-pound gorilla, but may be an average pussycat who wants nothing more than a glass of milk and a soft bed free from bother. Most bargaining takes place between people of different strengths, and this chapter deals with how you negotiate in the highly frequent case where you are dealing with equals-or-better and don't have any overpowering take-charge advantage which you can throw into the situation. In such bargaining, your tactics will have considerable importance in arriving at an agreement that meets the needs of both sides. There are fifteen guides which can help you achieve that outcome when you are dealing with equals or betters.

1. *Don't assume you know what the other side wants.* Often we act toward other people according to stereotypes in our minds. We think that the superrich are aloof and haughty, the poor are the cause of their own distress, and that employees only want less work and more pay. Yet if we take time to seek out individual differences, we may find that their interests are closer to ours than we had imagined, that they will

be more reasonable than supposed, and that their ogrelike image is not a true one. Finding out fully what the other person wants before you start a deal can come from advance research, or it may have to emerge through careful exploration during the negotiations.

Two travelers across the desert pulled into a small gas station and bar simultaneously from opposite directions and rushed into the bar. Each demanded a beer. The owner shrugged his shoulders and reported sadly that he only had *one can left*. The two customers began a shouting match, trying to persuade the owner and each other to sell it to them. Tired of the racket, the owner whipped out a huge pistol and laid it on the bar. "I am going to toss a coin and the winner gets the beer." He tossed the coin, one of the customers called heads, and it came up tails. The winner paid for the beer, then to the amazement of both witnesses opened it and poured the contents into the bar sink, stuck the can in his pocket, and walked out. "Just a minute, fella, what did you ever do that for?" asked the chagrined loser. "Oh, I didn't want to drink it. I am a beer can collector and I get some of my rarest and most valuable cans in out-of-the-way bars like this one," he replied as he drove away. A little more probing on both sides might have led to a happier conclusion.

You can't always assume that your interests in a bargain are the other side's. Constructing a NEEDS/WANTS portfolio and updating it during the negotiation will be helpful. Nothing is more fatal to your cause than to argue to a need that doesn't exist. Take the great debates about the emotional issue of abortion. It would be silly to argue that "it would save money" to choose pro-abortion or anti-abortion laws, when the parties are indifferent to such aspects, and the moral issues or pro-life and women's rights are the real wants.

2. *First offers are generally not accepted.* When you walk in with an equal or slightly better opponent and your first offer is flatly rejected, don't assume that all is lost and the other side has firmed up its position. First offers are usually rejected, but that merely opens the negotiation, not closes it. Making your first offer high thus is still a sound tactic, for the other side usually knows that your first offer is not final, and even if they laugh wildly or make contemptuous utterances about it, don't fold up and run. Keep selling the features and benefits of the offer, and perhaps start sweetening it to release signals that you are ready for some kind of counteroffer.

3. *Provide room to maneuver.* Start high if you are selling and low if you are buying, and always have a reason for the first offer. People will

often do things if they are given a reason, even if the quality of the reason isn't all that hot. A French professor of our acquaintance reported that she was having a problem with students not showing up for the last two classes of the semester. We suggested that she give the students a reason for coming, any reason. She complied with the suggestion. "If you don't come to class your mother will die," she soberly told the class. Shocked and amused, they chuckled, but *most of them came to the class.* If the reason is a sound one, better yet.

4. *Don't be modest in your demands* that the other side take full part in bargaining. Get all of the other side's demands on the table before you start conceding anything. Ask "yes, what else?" as he or she completes their side of the story. Restate their demands and indicate that you understand without accepting or rejecting. "I understand what you are saying, tell me more" is sound tactics. Keep pressing through this nondirective questioning until they have laid their full story before you.

5. *Get the other side to make the first concessions on major issues.* You can often do this by indicating that give-and-take negotiations are under way, and you are willing to move by making some concessions on minor points first to establish the idea that concessions are part of the game. Use the tools of logic and argumentation. From the checklist of tools explained in Chap. 8 you can rely on such logical tools as these:

- Appeals to authority ("That's probably conflict of interest").
- Analogy ("You are trying to bomb us".)
- Use better numbers ("Percentagewise we are stronger").
- Use the weight of dollars saved or lost ("We'll save you $9,600").
- Introduce printed evidence to back your case.
- Appeal to a larger audience ("The customers will love it").
- Appeal to the past ("We are old customers").
- Appeal to the future ("Our business will get bigger").

Inference is also a valuable logical tool when dealing with equals or betters in bargaining. If they say something very narrow and specific, expand it into a generalization which you infer from their words, and toss that back to them. "You ask for rights of inspection before acceptance. You are trying to come in and run our whole plant."

One party states that he finds it hard to believe a piece of information he has just heard. "Are you calling me a liar?" is a use of inference to produce a generalization. Inference means *widening* the argument from something very specific to a sweeping generalization, and has some valuable uses in getting the other side off your sparse facts and onto a defensive level. It is a way of changing the subject from something you might not want to have fully revealed to something which the other side would wish to deny.

To get the other side to make the first concession, you should have a pattern of logically based arguments which must be responded to by the other side. By logical argument you may get some concessions which by themselves aren't much, but it does keep the bargaining going.

6. *Don't make concessions cheaply.* Make the other side labor and sweat a little for every gain they win. Most people realize that there is no free lunch, and you shouldn't create the impression that you are an easy mark by casually giving away something of value. The expression "Whatever you say" should never be a reason for giving away one of your wants and needs. Even if you are giving away something you heartily desire to get rid of anyhow, get something in return.

A division manager received a call from corporate office and was asked if he could spare Mr. X from his staff to fill a minor staff position at corporate headquarters. It happened that X was a noted loser, a loafer, and the most ineffective member of the division manager's staff. Rather than divulge candidly his opinion, he decided to use this as a chip in some other requests he intended to make upon corporate office later that week. "X is like my right arm, chief. I want to be a good citizen and I will go along with your request because I am a company man, but you should know that this is a major concession we are making." The grateful boss, hearing confirmation of his opinion of the value of X, hastened to assure the division manager he was grateful "and that's one we owe your division, Joe." When the division manager had hung up the phone and notified X to start packing, he told his assistant, "We finally unloaded that lemon." An appreciative X was pleased at his apparent promotion and always favored his old division whenever something could be done from the elevated position he now held at corporate office.

7. *Give away straws, not the whole bale.* If you are convinced that some back-paddling on your part is needed, do so with small increments and evaluate how well each has worked before you give something else. It is sometimes sound to bundle up two or three small concessions to concede at the same time, then ask, "And what do you have to offer in return?" Give the other person the sensation of operating on an inclined

plane upward in the bargaining, even if the incline is a downslide or merely an intangible. You can stop being aggressive and start being charming, you can listen more attentively where previously you have feigned indifference or boredom. You can flatter them where you have been less that flattering before. You can smile and nod agreement at unimportant points. All of these trivial actions can be construed as a minor kind of concession to the other side. The concession doesn't have to be in dollars, but in moves which indicate a softening of your attitude and behavior. Even saying something like "I can't see anything wrong in that" can be a major concession. Use the word-splitting techniques of diplomacy, in which *understandings* come before *agreements in principle* and these come before *firm and final agreements*. It is better to time phase your concessions so that you agree first "in principle" before you concede the specific time, cost, quantity, quality, and service involved.

8. *Get something in return for every concession.* Two old Yankee farmers were trading over the price for one farmer boarding the other farmer's horse Nell.

"How much are you asking?"

"Ten dollars a week."

"Sounds mighty steep, how much will you take?"

"I'll take five."

"Humph. I see, but how much are you going to pay me for the manure you'll be getting from Nell?"

"For five dollars there ain't going to be any."

Every time you make a concession it should be costed out, and that sum added to the total cost of concesssions. In labor relations it has been a source of considerable loss to some firms who signed a bargain before they figured out the true cost of a concession that seemed quite simple and uncomplicated. *Never* concede anything in which the cost could be open-ended. Many employers during the seventies conceded to union demands that the company pick up the whole bill for health insurance premiums. The price at the time of bargaining was quite specific, and though high, it was reasonable. In the ensuing years, however, rising medical care costs produced rapid rises in health insurance premiums which the company was required to pay, and which proved to be an onerous bill, and added substantial costs which had to be passed along to customers in product prices. This made some products uncompetitive with those of foreign manufacturers who had no such costs. Higher wages can be traded for some flexibility of management of the work force which could make up the costs in improved productivity. Calculate the costs of every concession before you give it away, and get something which has a fair chance of balancing the concession.

9. *Keep a record of concessions and agreements on each side.* In managing by objectives, one of the persuasive reasons for setting objectives is to determine the level of bonus which will be paid at the end of the year. Many years ago Pete Estes, then manager of the Chevrolet division of General Motors, told a class of MBA's at Michigan about his negotiations with upper management about his goals for each year. "They give me forty objectives and I go over them one by one, and usually we agree, but if we don't, they have the final authority to set them. On the other hand, the goals are going to come back to haunt me at the end of the year when my bonus is figured, and since that bonus came to about $250,000 last year, I always make my own notes of everything that is said, both by me and them."

Lee Iacocca, the colorful former president of Ford and currently Chrysler Corporation, described his pattern to a reporter from *Time* magazine. "At the beginning of every year I sit down with every manager who works for me, and we talk about his goals for the coming year. We keep talking until we get an agreement, and I confirm it all in writing. He has a copy and I have a copy. At the end of each quarter we pull out those memos and talk once more about what he said he was going to produce and what he actually did." Those notes and the final agreement which it leads to are a vital part of the process of negotiation.

Have a recorder on your side who has a keen ear and can reproduce what has been conceded. This is more than a stenographic record, but a summary statement of concessions. A lot that goes on in negotiations isn't worth writing down, and the recorder should be a person who knows the difference between fluff and substance. These notes should be typed up daily and distributed to both sides. If there are understandings rather than agreements, they should be so noted. Exact wording must still come later. In some negotiations where the stakes are high it is not uncommon to have interim understandings typed up and both sides initial the typed agreement of understanding. This marks progress and formalizes slightly the idea that the sides are moving toward agreements.

The top negotiator should try to avoid being the recorder, for the task of writing notes may take his or her attention away from the sharpness of logic and debate, and the manipulating of information.

Using some kind of charting on a large sheet showing concessions, understandings, agreements, and agreements in principle can help the negotiator see the big picture. The chart should reflect every significant and most of the minor concessions.

10. *Set deadlines during the negotiations.* If you have offered to make a major concession, don't leave it dangling in mid air to be picked to death or die of exposure. Indicate that this is contingent upon some movement on the other side, and unless some counteroffers are produced by a specific time, you will have to "reconsider" the concession. It is perfectly okay to withdraw a previous offer if it was conditional, attached to a deadline for some counteroffer, and such offer fails to emerge within the time stated. "Our previous concession is apparently not going to produce a reasonable response and therefore please consider that offer withdrawn and inoperative as of now." Then proceed to something else. You haven't lost anything, for you have identified a possible place for them to trade a cncession later on.

11. *Always weigh concessions by yourself and the other side against needs and wants.* It is vital to keep in mind what you must not give and to be ready to trade with the things you are prepared to give. This means sorting out the transactions as they occur, and modifying your estimate of the other side's needs.

One large company's president had been captain of the Old Jade University hockey team when he was young, and each year urged the director of college recruiting to go to Old Jade and try to hire the captain of the hockey team. At Old Jade the word soon got out that being captain of the hockey team was tantamount to getting a choice job with plenty of opportunity at this firm. Soon the price for the student became higher and higher to the firm. The recruiters were cornered into offering choice assignments to the hockey captain's liking, a better than average salary, and some guarantees about job progress which ordinary students, however bright, were less likely to command. When the president eventually learned that his recruiter was offering bonuses, cars, and cushy jobs to a mediocre person, he came to his senses and lowered the "must hire" instruction to a mere "nice to have" category, which made it somewhat tougher on subsequent hockey captains at that school.

You should always examine your *must* objectives, and if you learn in negotiation that they are impossible, or are placing barriers that will be very costly, you should test those priorities hard to see if they really are all that important. Often, hiring requirements set by the data processing manager that "every computer programmer must be a college grad" can be impossibly difficult to negotiate, and you should question the priority.

12. *Avoid retroactive concessions.* Often in the pressure to make a deal we may see a one-time sweetener in the form of retroactive benefits. Labor contracts which settle for less than the union demanded may be achieved by making the increase effective backward from the time of the end of the contract. Take the case of a union contract which ended in June. The union demanded fifty cents an hour across the board, and the company offered fifteen cents an hour. As the time for expiration and a strike deadline loomed, they settled for 37½ cents, an exact split down the middle. At the last moment the union nibbled and waffled, and demanded that the raise be effective back to February 1. The company agreed, and found that they had eaten up a substantial amount of the profit for the last quarter, for they couldn't make prices to their customers retroactive. Any retroactive concession should be matched by offsetting benefits that more than compensate for the often unforeseen consequences.

Often, retroactive concessions entail something other than money, such as admission of wrongdoing, guilt or failure in the past, or past injustice. The American Indian Movement has been a leader in effecting some gigantic retroactive settlements for the misdoings of our ancestors. While one can applaud their negotiation skills, such concessions should be opposed in most negotiations. It is more productive to face the future, promise better things ahead, and sew them up with firm agreements. Liberals, says William F. Buckley, Jr., have a "passion for retroactive justice." Such cases, once started are endless.

13. *Four ways to get the other side to move first.* When you are confronted with a demand and you realize that your first offer won't stand up in the long haul, don't be the first to move if you can possibly avoid it. This is especially important in major items of contention, your "need" items. Research shows that the person who makes the biggest single concession first will end up worse off in the end.

- Use logic and argument to get the other side to move by destroying their case and building the features and benefits of your own.
- Rally information to build the merits of your own offer.
- Try making an offer for a few harmless items out of the whole offer by the other side. This is to take their whole package and try to find one or two subordinate parts which are attractive and offer to take those. This is like the shopper who goes into a store and buys

only the special-price loss leader items, then walks across the street to do the rest of his shopping.

- When they start to move, respond in kind, but less than theirs.

14. *Change the shape of the concession offer.* You can often get further concessions from the other side by sweeteners and side deals in lieu of price. These would include the following examples:

- "I will double the size of the order if you sell at the price I have offered."
- "I will make this a three-year rather than a one-year contract."
- Call your product a "system." This is the way military contractors often sweeten the deal with the government. Rather than selling guns and bullets, they call it a "ground offensive infantry combat system." They add a rash of manuals, special training courses, visual aids, ten days of consulting, and tack the label "system" on it. It can often double the sales price.
- Offer to level out the other side's production by accepting delivery in the slow season.
- Tie in orders to something else which they aren't selling especially well at this time.
- Offer reciprocal buying agreements where they are legal. "If we can get a good deal on your product, we will sell you our product at a discount."
- Advance payments and accelerated terms of payment can swing the vendor who is short of cash.
- Offering other services such as storage facilities, trucking, special processing, packaging to special specification, and generous return policies can produce concessions at times.

The cardinal rule here is to be sure you have consulted your accountant on each of these concessions to be sure that it is priced out very accurately, and that you aren't blowing the whole profit on the deal in order to get the contract.

If you can't win now, try to lock up a victory for the future. At one college campus, a religious foundation sends out letters asking members of the faculty to work on their projects. They are asked to respond by checking one of three choices:

___ I will take part in the above program now.

_____ Thank you but I am not interested in your organization and its purposes.

_____ Sorry I can't do it this year but will take part next year. Count on me then.

Being gentlemen and not wishing to appear either uncooperative or offensive, many check item three, and a year later are hooked.

15. *Don't be afraid to say no.* This is one of the major weaknesses of many negotiators, especially if they are amateurs and haven't learned the costly effects of trying to be agreeable. Because this is of major significance, the folllowing section explores that rule in more detail.

SAYING YES AND NO IN NEGOTIATIONS

It has been said that the only unforgivable speech defect is the inability to say no. Saying yes to things we shouldn't have has led to unhappy employees, bankrupt firms, miserable marriages, and years of debt. Why do we have such a propensity for saying yes when a simple "No" would have been so much more to our benefit?

- We hope to win approval and acceptance from others.
- We wish to be liked and want to avoid being the subject of anger.
- We try to avoid hurt feelings.
- We didn't anticipate the consequences in full.
- We want to put others in our debt.
- We see ourselves as "kindly."
- We think it is good manners or genteel.
- We fear conflict of wills.

A young supervisor in an auto parts plant was being treated with contempt by an older worker who often flouted orders, especially a safety rule which required that goggles be worn while grinding. One day the young supervisor's boss happened along, saw the older man grinding without goggles, and pointed out the violation.

"What are you going to do, Jim?" he asked.

"Well, I am just avoiding a fight," he explained.

"Not really—he has fought and won. Maybe he doesn't know it, but *you do.* Now go do your job."

The point here is that you can fall into the habit of saying yes when you should say no. When you say yes, verbally or tacitly, by condoning something you don't really want to, you build up your own resentment and anger. You have a right to define your own limits of generosity. The young supervisor subsequently practiced the art of saying no and meaning it.

When to say no. It is appropriate to say no to certain kinds of demands and offers in negotiations. Among them are the following:

- When the other side makes thoughtless or inappropriate remarks.
- When asked to do something for someone when they should do it for themselves.
- Requests which conflict with your own priorities.
- Committing others in your organization against their will.
- When a request conflicts with something you need and nothing is offered in compensation.
- When you know you can't deliver what is asked for.
- When you have been worn down by constant requests.
- When the other side gives you an unreasonable deadline and says, "Take it or you will miss out forever."
- When saying yes to the first step commits you to bigger and unacceptable commitments later on. (The camel's nose under your tent.)
- Before you have considered the options open to you.
- The first offer or demand.
- To small nibbling side conditions after the agreement is reached.

How to say no. The way you say no can be important in making it stick. Here are some proved ways of saying no:

- Do it promptly if you know what the final answer will be.
- Don't feel obliged to explain and justify every refusal.
- Don't say no impatiently or in anger. Using a soft "No" is very hard to rebut.
- Find a sounder proposal which has the effect of softening the answer.
- Show concern for the other person as an individual. Reject their ideas without rejecting them individually as persons.
- Demonstrate that you have heard what they have said, and restate their demand or proposal. "I understand your problem, which is that you have customer relations problems here. Now let me tell you my problem and why I am refusing your demand."

Caucus to determine the effects of yes and no to key proposals. It is often hard in the heat of negotiations to see all of the consequences to everyone involved in saying yes to something which has an air of plausibility about it, and which would seem to make great progress in negotiation. The most sensible idea is to caucus and review all of the possible consequences of saying yes or no. This may take time, but if the issue is important, the time is well spent.

One negotiating team uses the following "consequence chart" as a discussion guide to define the impact of alternative choices: saying yes or saying no. Using a chart pad, or several of them, get your team thinking about *all four squares.* You must list both the favorable and the unfavorable consequences of each position, yes and no. From this comes your decision, which should probably produce a counter which is neither a clear-cut yes or no, but is conditional. This helps shape your counterproposal to the offer or demand when you return to the table from your caucus. Not only should consequences to the negotiators be considered, but also consequences to the company, customers, vendors, employees, and the public.

THE HEIGHTENED IMPORTANCE OF LISTENING IN NEGOTIATIONS WHEN DEALING WITH EQUALS AND SUPERIORS

The skilled communicator has some distinct advantages in negotiations. The world authority on negotiation Gerald Nirenberg observes that despite all of the ostensible importance we attach to it, there is one aspect of communication in which we fail most often: listening. This

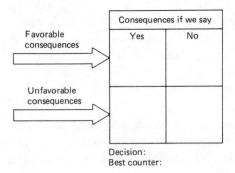

Figure 9-1. Caucus Work Sheet for Identifying Consequences of Other Side's Proposal.

requires concentrated attention to the other person, what is being said and his or her apparent emotional state. Manifestations of emotion as shown in stance, posture, facial expression, and eyes are what the sender sees in the receiver, and when such evidences are not focused upon the talker, the impression that listening is not occurring is clear. The other person in turn tends to become apathetic, bored, or angry, and to focus that condition upon the bored listener.

When a person in a negotiation has only a equal or poorer position, the most important successful tactic may be to listen with utmost concentration to what the other side is saying and expressing in behavior. *For it is out of the messages and signals from the superior party that you find the keys to winning.*

The model shown in Fig. 9-2 was developed by two scientists at Bell Telephone Laboratories to be a model for the communication process. For communication to occur, the sender (A) must first have some kind of idea and clarify that idea before expressing it. This intention of the sender is then converted into a code (B) of words, language, symbols, and messages which will then be transmitted (C) by such means as word of mouth, telephone, radio, newspapers, letter, or similar medium. At the other end of the scale, the receiver (E) must decode the message (D), and the result will be an understanding on the part of the receiver. To verify this message and correct its errors, the message is sent back and checked against intention in the feedback process (F).

While the original design of this model was to establish the theory of

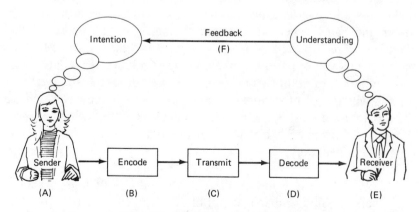

Figure 9-2. A Model for Communication.

communication for telephonic purposes, to other observers it became clear that this was likewise a model of considerable value in the social communication process. It helps us to see how listening can be improved in the negotiation process.

1. The good listener tries to dig out the intent of the sender even when it is expressed incompletely or incoherently.

2. The listener should be sure that the decoding ability on his or her side is equal to the coding ability on the sending side. ("What do you mean by that word?") *Definitions of terms* when an unclear word or expression crops up should be done immediately.

3. Communication then means "Behavior which produces an exchange of meaning," and not simply talking or writing.

4. While a great deal of the responsibility for communication, it is said, lies with the sender, achieving this perfection of sending may be difficult if the other person has a lower motivation to communicate than the listener. The very rich person talking to the beggar, unless he or she has some special qualities of empathy, may not see any special values in working hard at clarifying communication between them. Easier, just pass a coin (or write a check) and walk away.

5. When you are negotiating with one who has an equal or superior bargaining position, you have a special interest in making the communication process as close to perfect as possible, and this requires keen attention to what is being said. From incoming information you may find a key to changing their behavior, shaping agreements, and finding a basis for meeting your mutual needs.

Thirteen impediments to effective listening. Research into what makes for effective listening reveals the difference between good listeners and bad listeners. Such research shows that a number of bad listening habits are the key. If you can identify which of these bad listening habits you often fall into, you might, by practice and attention, eliminate some or all of them and increase your listening abilities. This in itself will arm you for those tough negotiations with equals which are the sort that are most apt to end up in deadlock. Check which of these thirteen bad listening habits you find are yours and start a corrective program immediately.

_____ *Do you speak before you think?* Many do. They hate the silence and possible embarrassment of awkward silence, and will utter anything to break it. This ruins listening.

___ *Do you make interruptions while others are talking?* Wait until the whole story unfolds before you make judgments or rebuttals.

___ *Do you think of something else?* Our minds have a capacity to think of several things at once, and the listening speed of most people is faster than the speaking speed of presenters. This makes it easy to let our minds wander, and we lose a key message from the other side. Concentrate on the sender.

___ *Are you overanxious to rebut?* When the other person is developing an argument, every point we hear impels us to leap in and deny its truth. Better wait until everything is out, then decide what is important enough to work on in rebuttal.

___ *Do you allow distractions from others?* People talking when the other side is presenting, rump conferences, and whispers distract from the process of listening. If your side wants to chatter, call a caucus. Don't allow distractions to stop you from hearing everything the other side says, even if it is repetitious.

___ *Do you brush off the other side's message* because it seems too technical or not familiar? Stick with them all the way. Ask for definitions and explanations of anything you don't understand, and repeat it all back to be sure they agree with your understanding.

___ *Do you jump to conclusions* before the whole story is told? The arrogant negotiator may feel he has heard it before, or say that it is like something else he has heard which was false, a party line, or the like, and leaps to a conclusion. Listening means tuning yourself in for *fine differences* in the other side's story. Watch for the tiny shades of difference which indicate some bending in your direction.

___ *Do you try to remember too much* and get lost? The other side may be presenting a complicated and lengthy story. Take notes. If you get lost, call for a halt, ask them to repeat, then restate back what you understand has been said, ask for confirmation, then urge them to go on. Don't leap across barriers of understanding blind.

___ Do you let your listening effectiveness fall by *focusing upon the appearance, delivery, language, or personality of the speaker* rather than the message? The union bargainer who used rough shop language was least listened to, for the other side, college grads all, were ruffled by this uncouth behavior and failed to listen. Similarly, appearing snooty, unkempt, too fastidious, supercilious, or even being overweight can turn some people off. Learn to ignore appearance. The message is more important than the container.

_____ *Is your span of attention short?* Many people simply can't concentrate on a single topic for very long or keep silent. They have to talk to ease their boredom. If you can't cultivate the patience to fix upon an important topic and stick with it for any length of time, don't get involved in negotiation. Send somebody who can.

_____ *Do you often discard information you don't like?* This is like the person who announced that she had been reading so much about the ill effects of cigarette smoking upon her health that she couldn't stand it any longer so she gave up reading. When we don't like something and throw it away for that reason, we have become terrible listeners.

_____ *Do you lack patience?* Some people lack patience in general— they are restless, finger-tapping, toe-stomping individuals. In other cases, people suffer fools poorly, or dislike people from other parts of the country, or people of different race, sex, or religion. Face the fact that you must allow for the effect such dislike will have on your listening effectiveness.

_____ *Do you fail to concentrate on ideas* and understanding them? We may listen for facts and figures only. While figures are important, there are more subtle issues which are just as important, and we must keep our attention tuned to understanding what the other's intent is, as well as their words and symbols.

Now go back through the list and check the ones in which you might improve. How many such areas did you find? If you have *over five* checks, you should try to find a good course in listening improvement, available through evening courses and adult education courses. If you have less than that, work out a planned program on your own to sharpen your listening skill to improve your dealings with people who are on a par with your or better.

LISTEN FOR INSIGHT

The point of this listening is that you will be listening for something special. You take it all in, filter it, and find the valuable tidbits which you can turn into a path to agreement. As you use good listening as a means of getting the other side to put forth their whole case, note some of the following:

- What does the other side need in this situation?
- What might they want in addition?
- How could we fill that need and still get to where we want to go?
- What would we have to trade to get to that balance of agreement? To get there you must constantly receive, then monitor what has come in, pick out of it the essentials which will be useful, and shape your strategy and tactics to use that information productively.

10
Negotiating from a Weak Position

"Now when we get there, I want vou to
come down front and stare at the man
and don't say nothing. You just glare."
—TOM WOLFE, *Mau Mauing the Flak Catchers*

Irwin Shaw in his novel *The Young Lions* tells of an American paratrooper whose jump in the dark had landed him in a giant tree behind
enemy lines. Hanging twenty feet off the ground by the lines of his
chute, he watched stolidly as a platoon of German SS troopers ran up
beneath him and looked up at him. The leader taunted him, asking him
if he had anything to say before he died. The paratrooper calmly
responded with a counteroffer: "I'll make you a deal, kraut face, if you
cut me down from here I'll accept your surrender and that of your men
and the war will be all over for you." Not everybody has the cool to
carry off such an audacious offer in their bargaining. How did the
trooper make out? You'll have to read the book to find out. The point
doesn't have to do with war, or paratroopers. but the ways you can do
your best when faced with a weak starting position.

Your position may be weak for any of a number of reasons:

- You are a tiny company dealing with a giant conglomerate.
- You have been caught in a recent case of bad work, poor delivery,
  wrong stock, or defective materials shipped, and now you are seeking to resume order taking.
- You are a subordinate to an autocratic boss who is quick to fire
  people who don't readily agree with his proposals and goals.
- You are trying to break in as a supplier to a large firm which has
  had a long-term arrangement with another big supplier with whom
  the customer is very pleased.
- Your product is either overpriced, of less quality, or a combination
  of the two.

- The other side has dozens of options and you are but one of those options. You need them and they don't need you.

The list could go on endlessly: You have weak credit; you lack the experience and reputation to do the job you are seeking; you have recently been caught with your hand in somebody's cookie jar and your reputation is tainted. It would be very easy to blow the negotiations with a single inept action. Yet you do have an advantage *if the other person is willing to meet and talk to you.* Even if it simply a perfunctory session, or just a courtesy gesture, it affords you a chance to gain something you need and start back up again from the bottom.

The first and most important set of rules for such cases are negatives: *things you should avoid* at all costs in such sessions. Here are some of the tactics you should avoid like poison:

Rule 1: *Don't complain, don't explain.* We often start out with the assumption that the other person is dead set against us and knows more about our weaknesses than he or she actually knows. If you enter the room with an apologetic air, and start immediately to explain how the situation got you caught short, and complain about past injustices that have been done you, the meeting will probably be short. Of course if the other side brings up something that weakens you, you have a terse, firm, logical, and very positive explanation of the situation, but get off it as quickly as you can and turn to the future.

In 1943 one of the authors was an officer in an Army camp in the South. Over the weekend one of the men in his company had gone to town, gotten drunk, torn up several bars, insulted the flower of Southern womanhood in a very gross fashion, fought with several military policemen, stolen a jeep, and finally had been overwhelmed by a platoon of MP's who had dragged him back, battered and torn, to his company, where he presented himself on Monday to his commander for discipline. The officer read the rap sheet aloud as the woebegone excuse for a soldier stood before him. Having finished the list, he then stared at the culprit and asked, "Now, soldier, what have you to say for yourself?"

"Captain," he said, smiling deferentially, "my girl is coming to town next weekend, and I was wondering if you could see your way clear to give me a three-day pass?" The outcome of course was not what he requested, but his utter gall and the panache with which he presented it struck a responsive chord, and his punishment was limited to confinement and a stern lecture. In time the story became a company legend and evoked ever-enlarged versions of how many MP's he had whipped single-handed, the stolen jeep had turned into a tank, and it was falsely asserted that he had become the favorite of many women who had been insulted by him.

Avoiding defensiveness is one of the cardinal rules of negotiating from a weak position, and if your case is absolutely hopeless without a shred of merit, a stylish offensive may at least embellish your reputation for the future.

Rule 2: *Avoid admissions and confessions.* A prominent psychological consulting firm frequently retained to interview candidates for employment in a large firm has a favorite question of applicants. After first providing the candidate a chance to describe his major strengths in detail, they then pop the loaded question: "You apparently know yourself quite well, sir. What would you say are a couple of your *major weaknesses?*" Only a damn fool who didn't really want the job very badly would ever hand his adversary such a weapon. It would be like a fighter standing in mid ring with his arms at his side suggesting to his opponent, "If you see an opening, hit me." If the stakes are high and the opponent a professional, he will land a punch that will leave only one question open, whether you get knocked out of the ring through the ropes, or over them. Faring far better were those applicants who described some highly desirable trait as their "weakness." For example, one said, "My major weakness is that I am a workaholic. I simply don't know how to quit and enjoy a personal life, I get so obsessed with my work." Another confessed that "I am really too ambitious, and that drive to do a job and get ahead is my obsession." The interviewer always noted these as strengths.

Confession, while sometimes good for the soul, may be bad for the body, the car it rides in, the house it owns, and the size of its bank account. Three men of the cloth agreed to a mutual confession session one day. The Catholic priest sheepishly admitted that from time to time he overindulged in sacramental wine. The Methodist minister admitted to having regularly overstated his travel expense account. The third, a Presbyterian, paused briefly, then confessed: "My problem is that I am an inveterate and incurable gossip, I am always running off at the mouth, and can hardly wait to get out of here to tell what you fellows have said."

Rule 3: *Never attack the stronger party personally.* Strong people and big men, it is said, are seldom rough on underlings and lesser people as long as their authority and influence aren't challenged by them. Start by conceding their stronger position. Even a bit of flattery which exaggerates that power somewhat won't usually do much harm, for it indicates clearly that you do not intend to threaten them. Bosses, it is likewise noted, tend to view subordinates' behavior toward them in the light of how it makes them *look to their boss.* End runs threatened, or attacks which imply that the other side could be damaged through further dealings, will bring the dealings to a prompt end.

A Navy chief petty officer was explaining life raft procedures to some recruits in the event their ship sank. His advice was to hunker down in the life raft and attract as little attention as possible since the waters through which they would be sailing were alive with sharks. One young sailor nervously suggested, "Should we try to fight a shark off with our pistols, Chief?" Scornfully the chief spat to one side and replied, "Never! If you do you may get him pissed off." When you are dealing with Jaws himself, don't trigger any fierce response on the creature's part. Depend upon his being well fed, curious, and perhaps undergoing a quiet spell until he goes away. Then you can start cautiously paddling toward the nearest land, or await rescue.

Rule 4: *Never be dishonest, and don't surrender.* Don't try to be a wise guy when you haven't the votes, guns, troops, or supplies for a battle. A graduate student at the University of Utah owned a Porche and was addicted to driving well over the speed limits yet got fewer tickets than expected. His tactic, which deferred the ultimate day when he was grounded for a year, was to always cast his eyes *downward* when the trooper finally pulled him over and asked for his driver's license. "A Porsche is a very expensive car, and when these troopers pulled me over they probably expected some rich kid who was arrogant and overbearing. When I averted my eyes, was unfailingly polite, called him Sir and Officer, they always changed their tune a little bit." This appeared to work best with younger officers whose confidence in their importance was possibly lowest. It was finally a couple of old experienced troopers who were not taken in by the deferential manner who ticketed him solidly and grounded him.

Don't surrender. Deference—at least the avoidance of being pushy—plus persistence has some distinct advantages in negotiating with the overpoweringly heavy opponent. Persistence—refusal to quit—is especially valuable, for its distinguishes you from other people, most of whom will be put off by a rejection when they are convinced from the start that they can't win. The negotiator who keeps returning to the table with the same story but with another new piece of evidence is very apt to win over the person who gives up too easily. There are some rules for using persistence, however:

1. Always be cheerful along with your persistence, and avoid hostility.

2. You can often make persistence a virtue by putting a short time limit on successive interventions. Many a salesman has captured a customer through a series of persistent requests for business, perhaps with some tactic like "All I need is five minutes of your time—five minutes."

3. You might find out what is the best time to get onto the schedule of another. Perhaps they arrive early, lunch at a special place, or ride on a certain commuter train. Taking time to find this out can produce open time to intervene with another sales pitch.

4. Always have *something new* to say on each successive petition. "I thought you might have missed the story in this week's *Times* which has a bearing on what we were discussing in our last session."

5. Indicate that you respect their time and will help conserve it by making your story brief. Keep going back.

6. Show that you remember what the other side said the last time, and in the past, and use it in subsequent sessions.

7. Never deprecate yourself with such utterances as "Here I am, that pest again." You may be planting an idea that doesn't exist. Speak the language of success and opportunity. "Just one more chance to tell you another valuable reason you might want to consider our side of the story"

When confronting a tough and stronger opponent, this piecemeal negotiation may be the only way you can get the job done. You might otherwise be given a brush-off: "I have ten minutes, then I have to do something very important." The other side is thus telling you that you aren't all that heavy in their eyes. If the time allotted is too short, don't terminate negotiations, but ask for another opportunity some time later. *Don't adjourn, recess.* Then you can keep popping back for five and ten minutes or half-hour shots—friendly, persistent, and never backing down. Underlying your whole approach with your better-armed opponent must be a strong streak of sincerity. Indicate that you take him seriously. What makes for sincerity?

1. Never get clubby and call the other by an overly familiar nickname. Generally stick to Mr. Jones until he specifically invites you to call him by his first name.

2. Don't volunteer a lot of personal information about yourself, your wife and kids, your mistress, your accountant, or your guru. The other party isn't on your side yet. Strictly business.

3. Avoid any evidence of immaturity or irresponsibility on your part, but rather aim at showing that you are concerned about the job at hand, the future, serving the other side's needs, and delivering quality and quantity of work on time. Avoid things which could mark you as immature, being excessively pleasure-minded, reckless, irresponsible, a heavy drinker, can't hold a job, and other kind of revelations which could mark you as one who shouldn't be trusted too far.

4. Avoid buying the other side tangible gifts if they have all of the power and you have little. Unless you are going to engage in a bribe, which can backfire terribly, it's better to leave gift-giving out of negotiation.

With these basic rules of what to avoid in negotiating when you are in a weak position, what then do you do? What affirmative actions are to be recommended? You choose a mixture from 35 major factors which negotiators report they have employed in such dealings. Not all of them will work in every case, and some of them are mutually exclusive. This list, however, does provide you a menu of tactics from which you can shape your own, picking the best. How can you tell which is best? This can be illustrated in Fig. 10-1.

The weaker bargainer has an urgent problem of doing the following things:

1. Size up your own needs and wants.

2. Try to find what possible needs and wants the other side might have.

3. Monitor the other's behavior during every moment of negotiation and adopt a strategy for finding agreement which meets the needs of both.

4. Choose appropriate tactics from the 35 tactics listed below. Then execute. Since you are constantly monitoring the other side, you note quickly which tactics receive a good response and which are rejected.

The portfolio of *needs and wants* explained in Chap. 6 becomes even more important when you lack strength against the other than it is when you are the dominant party. Remember, you have needs and wants, some of which are high and others low. So does the other side.

1. Those needs and wants which are *both low* are the things you wish to avoid by all means. You neither want nor need to be thrown out of

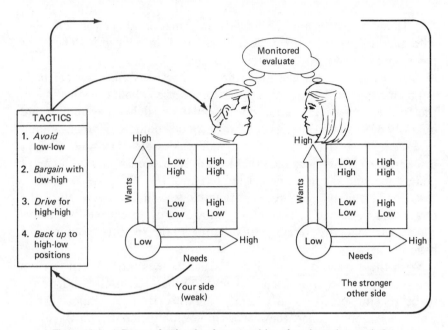

Figure 10-1. A Pattern for drawing from a position of weakness in negotiation.

the session without achieving anything, with future possibilities of another hearing ended permanently. This means that you must identify what are the low-low combination of needs and wants for the other side. When you are dealing with the powerful, they don't need to give you what you need, nor do they want to be personally embarrassed, annoyed, or insulted. This is the basis of the four rules of what to avoid which were listed earlier.

2. *The ideal outcome* (your bargaining objective) is to gain those things that you want and need and find some way of helping the other side achieve what it wants and needs. This is the ultimate level of success in your strategy and tactics.

3. There are things which you want very much, but you really could live without them. These are your *bargaining chips*. Give away some of the things you want in order to get the things you need, if necessary. Tie these chips together with an ingratiating style.

4. In the lower right hand corner of your portfolio are those things you highly need, but would prefer not to go that route. Perhaps you need the money, but wouldn't like to be caught in a bind with a sole customer

or supplier. You will take it if it is the only way to settle, but this is a backup position, not a main objective.

In dealing from weaknesses, your situation often comes from an inability to get behind the scene with the other side and find out what they really need. You will be better off, however, if you take the information you have gathered before the bargaining session and also during the negotiation through *questions and concentrated listening* to what the other side is saying and doing. Keep correcting your assessment of their portfolio as the meetings progress.

You are now ready to choose the specific tactical weapons for your negotiations. Remember that you will adapt, change tactics, and reverse yourself upon occasion when your monitoring shows that a tactic isn't working and threatens your objective (high, high). Here are the 35 tactics. You may add others as the negotiations emerge.

THINGS YOU SHOULD AVOID (THEY WILL FURTHER WEAKEN YOUR POSITION)

1. *Don't complain, don't explain,* you may be telling more than you should.
2. *Avoid admissions and confessions.*
3. *Never attack the stronger party.* Deference can help.
4. *Don't surrender, be persistent.*

HOW TO USE YOUR BARGAINING CHIPS

5. *Protect your needs* by giving away some items you would like to have but could get along without.
6. *Use your personal charm* and good manners to flatter the other side. This costs you nothing and may meet their wants and even some of their needs.
7. *Establish your credibility.* Even though it isn't smart to admit things unfavorable to yourself without reason, if you are confronted with some indisputable facts which you would prefer not to reveal, admit them if pressed hard. Don't get caught in errors of fact. "Yes, it's true that we do have a cash flow problem, but we intend to stay in business, and your contract could be vital to those plans, Mr. Jones. We are well managed and think we have a sound plan for succeeding." Keep your credibility high.

8. *Look and act smart at all times.* Be well dressed, at least be neat and businesslike. Never show up tired, smelling of liquor, or showing boredom.

9. *Do favors for the other side.* Offer personal favors, and tasteful help. Be willing to postpone if the other side requests it, but always ask for a specific date for reconvening. Without fawning, be helpful, courteous, and thoughtful of the other person.

10. *If you have any affiliations, stress them.* Tell the other side about other firms whom they might respect who use your ideas or services. Cite common acquaintance. If you can get letters of recommendation from people who are well connected with the other side, have them sent in advance. Use references and connections fully. Tell of common memberships, college connections, children attending the same school, and similar affiliative statements which would produce a sense that you have something in common.

11. *Be sincere at all times.* Make it clear that you take yourself seriously; don't tell jokes that would imply a familiarity you don't really have; no clubbiness. Make it clear that these negotiations are important to you. Be prompt in your appointments, and make your entry to the meeting place businesslike. There may be times when being flip, smart, or tough is best, but not now. You are the weaker party, remember. Play it straight arrow all the way.

12. *Read your opponent's signals carefully.* This is a time for trying out your course in body language, facial expressions, and other behaviorial cues from the other side. Read their intentions by watching their pose. If they start turning away, make moves that will keep their attention. Remember, you have to keep bargaining, and if you are really weaker they may simply walk away bored. They have lots of options, and you need them more than they need you, so watch for storm signals—irritation and the like. Don't send your resident rough guy to do the negotiating when you are the much weaker party. There is one exception to this: If the other side is a roughneck, the only person he might understand is your own rough guy.

Many years ago the customer relations department at American Can Company had a representative to deal with customer complaints, a very elegant chap who had attended St. Paul's prep and Harvard College. His dress, language, and style reflected his breeding. Unfortunately, one of the customers was a large brewery in Newark which bought billions of beer cans. This particular rep fared very badly. One day he was on vacation and the president of the brewing company was bawling over the phone for somebody to come over and listen to his complaints about poor quality tin cans being sent him. Since there was nobody else available, they sent the production manager of the beer cans. He was a tough manufacturing type whose language, appearance, and manners had been shaped on the production lines of Jersey City, New Jersey. Immediately when he walked into the brewery president's office, he said something like this:

"Listen, you bastard, I have been hearing second hand about your screaming and yelling and I think it's about time you heard the facts of life. You don't do any advance planning and when you need cans from us you want them all at once. We have to add three shifts in a single day! Do you realize what it takes to hire three complete shifts of production crews? We have to break them in, get them on the job, and try to teach them to run a high-speed can line that's running at 500 cans a minute? That's over 250 people in a single day! If you would start doing some planning and start ordering like a sane man, we wouldn't have to produce junk for the first week, and until you get your rotten act cleaned up I think you should quit your goddamn complaining about it to us. I personally am fed up to my ——— with your dictatorial crap, and I hope the hell you try to find another supplier today. Now what the hell else is on your mind?"

A huge grin spread over the ugly visage of the brewer, who now for the first time understood the production problems. "Where the hell has the can company been hiding you, sweetheart? Maybe we can work something out now that they have that fancypants from Harvard out of the way. Let's have a look at our schedule for the next couple of months." From that time forward, whenever there was a complaint, the brewer put through a call directly to his new-found buddy and got some straight answers in the language of the shop floor, which he spoke with considerable relish.

Normally, however, such a roughneck wouldn't be the best person to send on a diplomatic mission. The key ingredient here was the advanced production schedules. Once these schedules were released in advance, the timing of hiring and training new crews was smoothed out and the problems of poor quality disappeared.

PUTTING FORTH YOUR MAXIMUM EFFORT

Some issues which are high on both your need list and your want list also may be high on the other side's needs and wants list, and the differences may be the margin which fixes success or failure. It is this area where your best bargaining and negotiating tactics should be wheeled out. Here are some of the ways to deal when seeking these high-high items and you are the weaker party.

13. *Present an avalanche of facts.* Pull out all stops in giving the results of your prior research. Show the features and benefits of your case. Cite statistics, historical evidence, past experience, testimonials of other customers, and if you have the facts of how all this fits the other side's needs and wants, present them.

14. *Privately construct a range of acceptance levels.* You will be better off to set three levels of acceptance for proposals from the other side, and as a schedule of demands:

- The highest possible level hoped for—start with this.
- A good level where you could be quite satisfied.
- Your lowest or walk-away level.

Start with a spirited pitch for the highest level as your opener. Play it to the hilt and don't back down easily. Then if pressed and deadlocked concede the middle level or something in that direction. If all seems lost, before you walk out admitting defeat, move to the lowest level and make it clear that this is your last-ditch offer.

A student was working one summer selling brushes and applied this technique to selling on doorsteps with considerable success. His first attack was to try to sell the top of the line, vacuum cleaners and other high-ticket items. If after considerable bargaining this continued to be headed for a deadlock and no sale, he moved to the next set of items in the middle of the line. He offered deals, made added offers. "I'll mow your lawn free if you take this order" often won the day and created a permanent customer. He seldom mowed a lawn, but it did persuade many a motherly figure that he was determined and willing to work hard. His last-stop position was to sell them a toothbrush for under a dollar. "I never left without selling at least a toothbrush," he replied.

15. *Offer them a surprise they will like.* You can differentiate yourself from other negotiators if you can generate a creative and imaginative proposal which catches them off base and often will lead to an agreement. Many years ago one of the authors was working one summer with a crew of salesmen selling magazine subscriptions door to door to pay his way through college. Jobs were scarce, and the money was good for the top sales people. One hot August day in Ohio the youngster

approached a prosperous farmhouse and tried to sell subscriptions to some farmers' magazine to the owner of the farm. Obviously not interested, the farmer finally made a move to break off the discussion. "I have a horse that died and I have to bury him," he said, and turned away. "Wait a minute, I'll help you bury the horse." The farmer was surprised. "You will?" "Sure, it won't cost you a cent and all you have to do is buy some subscriptions, at least ten dollars' worth." The rest of the afternoon he dug the hole alongside the farmer, together they amputated the poor dead beast's legs and rolled the carcass into its last resting place. As they were prying the beast into the hole it was apparent that the farmer never could have done it by himself. "By gosh, young feller, I want to buy more than ten dollars' worth. Why don't you wash up and stay for supper. Then I'll make some phone calls and see if some of the other farmers around here wouldn't like to subscribe to some of them magazines too." The story of the horse and the young salesman's labors was recounted in considerable detail, and doors along the country road opened wide when he arrived.

16. *Offer some variety.* If you are suffering a weak position because of price, you have to employ what economists call "nonprice competition." You have to take what seems to be an ordinary deal and spice it up with some variety. A journalism graduate was applying for his first job as a reporter, but was the least experienced of those applying. "I want somebody who can write good and who can also write fast," the tough old editor declared. " Well, sir, I'll tell you something, I am faster than the better writers, and a better writer than those who are faster." The editor, taken by this variation of the product, hired him. "If you can write as slick as you talk, I think you are my man," he explained.

17. *Concede certainties.* "Sure it is true that IBM has a larger service organization than ours, but we are so small we have to show more personal attention to each customer." This concedes what the other side knows to be perfectly true, and admits a commonly known fact, then tries to turn it into an advantage.

18. *Stall for time.* If a particular line of discussion has been going badly, and the other side seems ready to come to an adverse decision, change the subject quickly and start wheeling along a new track. "Let's come back to terms of payment, which I think you should know will give you the use of your cash for a longer period of time than any other vendor."

19. *Keep control of the evidence.* In one merger negotiation between two banks, the issue at hand was the respective value of the two stocks

of the companies. The larger bank's representative went to the board and wrote down the respective profit figures of the two banks, showing that the smaller target bank had done quite poorly in that area the past year. The president of the smaller bank immediately went to the board and erased those figures before they could be fixed in everyone's mind and wrote another list of figures, showing use of assets which was much more favorable for his side. For several minutes he dwelled on this statistic, talking about its promise and significance, leaving it on the board when he finished. Be very cautious about letting members of your own side introduce evidence unless you are sure it will be favorable. Often an impulsive volunteer on your side will throw in the crucial bit of evidence which will destroy your case. This happens through inadvertence, not malice.

20. *Criticize the other party without hostility.* It isn't entirely wrong to criticize the other side, even though you are the weaker party, if you do it without hostility. It can be done in a sincere and straightforward way, using facts to justify the criticism. "The reason our performance hasn't been up to your standard in many cases, I am afraid, is because you never once let us know what those standards are. Certainly if we knew them we would have lived up to them without fail." Such an objective and straightforward statement often clears the air and swings a decision.

It is only when you realize that things are completely ripped to shreds that you make a desperation move and attack the other side personally. Lawyers have a saying that if you have a strong case, stress the facts, if you have a weak case, appeal to emotion. If you have no case at all, attack the prosecuting attorney. It should be noted that such tactics work only if the judge is naive or the jury is an emotional mob. When all is lost, however, and nothing else could be lost, you may shake up the situation and start movement through a personality attack on the other side. Remember, though, that you may be barring future reversals, hope of some recanting, and any chance of staging a comeback.

21. *Threaten to go over the head of the other negotiator.* Every time you enter negotiations you should make a quick judgment to classify the person on the other side of the table. This "DIP" rating tells you whether you are dealing with:

D—for decider
I—for initiator
P—for permitter

The decider is the best one to bargain with, for if you have an agreement it sticks and is final. An initiator is a person who can recommend your case to a higher level but can't make the decisions. The permitter is one who can allow you to go see the person who will decide but has nothing to do wwith the decision. The only issue to be negotiated by the permitter is whether or not you should be allowed past the outer office.

- If you are faced with a decider, stick tight and negotiate and negotiate. If he or she really is a decider, it's pointless to try to go over their head. If there is some higher authority figure and they have their wits about them, they'll endorse what their decider has decided and show you the door promptly.
- An initiator should be sold hard to join you in persuading that veiled figure above, the decider. You must persuade the initiator first, then use a coalition with that one to go to the next level. Clearly you need to go over the person's head, but you take him or her along.
- The permitter shouldn't be insulted, or turned into a foe, but if necessary you can make an end run with impunity around this one. The most affirmative answer possible from the permitter is "You may go in now." If you can get there on your own, go ahead.

22. *Get help from others.* If you are a weaker party, you can help your situation by bringing along your big brother, a lawyer, an expert, a connection, or a reference. Use any help you can get, seek out coalitions and supporters, backers and endorsers. Use people who have gone along with you before who would state their pleasure with your work.

A young second lieutenant in the Marines was faced with his first platoon assignment—a very large, tough, experienced troop of old marines. Sensing their scorn, he challenged them: "Do any of you people think you could whip me in personal combat, man to man?" The amazed platoon just stared, but one large and ferocious-looking private said, "I think I could take you, sir, if you'll just remove those lieutenant's bars." Throwing the bars in the dust, he walked up under the nose of the huge man. "Says who?" he said defiantly. "Well, sir, I am heavyweight boxing champion of the U.S. Marines," the man said. "Fine, you are hereby appointed platoon sergeant in charge. Now does anybody in this platoon think he is man enough to lick me and the new platoon sergeant?"

If you can get the strength of the other side to lean back against itself, you do even better. Find allies, make coalitions, and enlist good follow-ers—all will help in negotiation with stronger people than yourself.

23. *Call in experts.* Everybody respects an expert, and if your word is doubted or apt to be questioned, line up experts who have studied the case fully and can bring the fruit of their learning, study, and experi-ence to verify your side of the story.

24. *Appeal to law or government.* A small medical supply firm was trying to work out a commercial arrangement with a larger firm, but was getting nowhere. Faced with apparent indifference and a deadlock and end of the negotiations, they introduced their lawyer, who declared that in his opinion as an antitrust lawyer a failure to arrive at the requested arrangement would probably constitute a restraint of trade, and thus make the larger firm subject to a law suit under the Sherman and Clayton Acts. He cited prior cases which were similar. The larger firm calmly caucused, talked to their lawyer, and came back the next day and settled favorably.

In labor negotiations, appealing to the National Labor Relations Board, filing unfair labor practices charges, and similar ploys are famil-iar. These are always worthy tactics to have in reserve when dealing with a stronger side.

25. *Accept a partial settlement and try again later.* There is a very powerful effect to asking the other side to "at least give something. Don't send us away empty-handed. Throw us a bone." If you are per-sistent, this argument is often irresistible. This opens the gate through which you may come again for an enlargement of your share. In your first bargaining session it is very sensible to try for such an opening wedge. It doesn't hurt your competitors, and gives the other side a chance to show agreement without significant inconvenience.

26. *Appeal to his mercy.* Throwing yourself on the mercy of a pow-erful opponent will often help you get part of what you want, unless he has been thoroughly enraged or wishes to deny your plea on the basis of principle. If you are one of those cases in which you must be made an example of, then it won't work. The basis of this appeal is that it acknowledges the power of the others, flatters the other side by conced-ing their authority and their right to decide, and makes it clear that you are neither a threat nor an opponent but a would-be disciple. It gives the other side a chance to win another follower, which wise people will seize.

27. *Play the game like a chess game.* One of the tenets of chess is that the winner is the one who, barring dumb mistakes, commands the

center of the board early and holds it. Try to find the key issue and win your points there. You may then sacrifice some pawns or even trade pieces, always thinking several moves ahead.

28. *Play the infantry motto.* The Army infantry, the men who fight on the ground with rifles, bayonets, and machine guns, have as their official song "Take the high ground and hold it." Find a place where you have an advantage, however slight, capture that ground early, and hang tight to it. Fight to the last person before retreating from that high ground. First you must figure out what the high ground is for you, and dig in.

29. *Use skillful cross examination constantly.* The art of cross examination should be studied and employed when you are faced with a stronger party. The gist of cross examination is to let the other person's answers make *your case.* You shape your questions with the expectation that an answer favorable to you will come forth, which means that you must hve some knowledge of their past practices and policies. "You say that we are too small to handle a deal this size. Tell me, Mr. Smith, does your company have *any* small suppliers?" Of course they have small suppliers. They are proud of it. They will answer in the affirmative, which makes your case that you are not too small, and that smallness is an irrelevant argument, for they have already admitted it in their answer.

30. *Ask If-Then questions.* Using hypothetical questions is a way of obtaining concessions in the abstract which can often be turned into real concessions. "If we were to prove that we have a major bank that would lend us ample working capital, then would we appear to be more attractive as a supplier?" This would be in response to an argument that "You may not be big enough to handle a deal this big."

BARGAINING TO YOUR BACKUP POSITION

Certain kinds of objectives in negotiation have a split character. They would meet your needs, but you really wouldn't prefer them—in fact they don't meet your wants at all. For example:

- A dealer offers to buy your product but insists upon special packaging, special credit terms, or having an exclusive in a territory which would bar you from selling to others. You hate the last condition.

- Your boss agrees that you should be promoted but would like to add a heavy travel schedule to your responsibility. You would like the higher pay of the new job (in fact you need it badly), but the travel is distasteful.
- The union agrees to accept your pay offer, but wants it tied to a clause which gives the stewards paid time off for handling union business. You need the price agreement but would hate having the stewards doing their job on company time.

Here are some tactics you might draw on to achieve these objectives:

31. *Split the issues and bargain for each separately.* You should try to make them two separate issues. Seek an agreement on the one you need, and then disconnect the issue you don't want.

32. *Downgrade the connection through rumors.* Often there is a useful third party accessible to both sides with whom you can plant rumors. While rumors are not always useful, they could help disconnect the issues. You may plant the rumor that your advertising budget is bigger in areas where distributorships are not exclusive. You don't want to use this in direct rebuttal, for it may become an agreement you won't like. Rumors are an indirect unofficial form of argument. It makes the argument without entering it into the record. It interjects a rebuttal without being officially presented. This one takes skill, timing, and some luck.

33. *Play for home-field advantage.* Trial lawyers often ask the court to rule that the location of the trial (venue) be changed to another court. The reason for changing is to remove a local advantage that the other side has in the first court. You may find that picking the site of the negotiating can help you with matters which you wouldn't want to concede. Being on your own court with your own crowd yelling, and your own ref, close to your own records and facilities, has a real but hard-to-pin-down advantage. Often your physical plant, offices, and people comprise a background for negotiation which is persuasive to others. If on the other hand your home field is modest and your desire is to impress people that the opposite is true, meet on their grounds or rented neutral territory. This site question is often an area which you want but don't really need, however, and you should trade for the site as well as more substantive issues.

34. *Use the basketball maneuver called the "pick."* In basketball when a sharp-shooting, hard-driving forward is being guarded closely like plaster by a tenacious guard, he may try to use a "pick." He drib-

bles across the floor followed by the tormenting guard, but in his path one of his teammates takes a firm stance. Dribbling closely past his teammate, he scrapes off the guard, who may in his concentration on his target run into the "pick" and draw a foul. In negotiation you can try to pick off the issue you don't want from the one you need. Show the benefits of the thing you want, but dump disadvantages and disfavor all over the idea you wish to scrape off, and do it naturally in such a way you don't lose the main item you need.

35. *Be candid about your dislikes.* Occasionally it may have some value to state that you like the item which you need, but that you have a personal preference against the attached condition. If the other side is ready to agree on the big item from your view, they may be willing to drop the item which you expressed distaste for, simply because they learn that you don't like it. There is some advantage in getting them to know what your preferences are as well as what you need. They will try to bargain for something else as a substitute which you suggest.

SUMMARY

These thirty-five tactics cover many of the weapons which you can bring to bear in negotiation. There are of course others which can be used, or even better, invented by the skilled negotiator. Remember that they are to be used as follows:

1. Construct a portfolio of wants and needs for yourself.

2. Construct a portfolio of wants and needs for the other side as you size them up before the negotiations begin.

3. Keep amending them as you get information during the bargaining.

4. Keeping the four elements of the portfolio in mind, use those tactics which fit your bargaining portfolio of objectives.

The test of the experienced negotiator is to play his or her cards well, not count on the luck of the draw.

Still another vital aspect of your bargaining tactics is that of managing timing. That's what the next chapter deals with.

11
Timing—The Dynamic Dimension in Negotiation

In the early 1960s the professional football season was winding down with the Detroit Lions and the Baltimore Colts battling for the league championship. With three seconds to go in the game, Baltimore was two points beind and stymied on their own fifty-yard line. To the amazement of everyone they sent in their field goal kicker, a stalwart named Dempsey, and lined up for a field goal. Everyone in the stadium and in the living rooms around the country smiled knowingly and predicted a fake kick with probably a hang-it-up-and-pray pass. To the shock of everyone, Dempsey did kick it and furthermore placed it squarely between the goal posts to win the game. A classic moment in sports, this kick gained its greatest significance in its *timing*. If Baltimore had been ahead by thirty or behind by thirty points, the long kick might still have been a significant statistic. But the timing of the kick made it epochal in the sports record books.

Similarly in negotiation, timing of events can have as important a bearing as the abilities of the winning side. Not only do the actions you take affect the outcome, but also the sequence in which they occur. The quip which eased tension can be seen as an act of abominable taste if uttered at another moment. The use of patience—and impatience—is valued by its timing and position in the negotiation. Because timing is dynamic, and negotiations are time-phased transactions, no fixed set of rules will cover this key area of negotiation—only some precepts and generalizations drawn from experience. Twenty-three such precepts comprise the rest of this chapter. Here are some guides to management of timing in negotiation.

1. *Recognize that negotiations are time-phased.* Unlike golf or baseball, it is the last inning alone that determines the winner in negotiation.

Mistakes made in the early stages may be turned into advantages, which if made later could produce disaster. If you can set the time schedule for events, rather than being manipulated by others' time choices, you have a towering advantage. Negotiation of labor contracts by law must be held "at mutually convenient times and places," and this is a sensible guide. You must insist that the times for you be convenient, and the place be acceptable, or you have given away a crucial leverage.

2. *Think through in advance what the deadlines are.* If you have a requirement to settle in one week and the other person doesn't have any such time pressure, you have lost an advantage. Delay of negotiations when you have such a deadline and the other side does not works against you.

In the canning business in southern New Jersey the tomato pickers' unions have always worked hard to make sure the labor contract expires just as the tomatoes are ripening on the vine. Faced with a mountain of tomatoes which need packing or they begin to rot, the firm is under more pressure to settle. The company would prefer the expiration date to fall in the middle of the winter. You have some key times in your affairs when timing becomes crucial; deadlines occur. Try to avoid being cornered by those deadline times, by moving negotiations as far from that time as possible. You lose the power of timing if you can't wait the other side out on occasion.

3. *Do the small things first.* In planning your agenda it's best to make sure that a goodly handful of easy items show up early in the negotiations. This allows progress, which is a time-centered idea. Progress, says Webster, is forward movement in space and time. You enter negotiations not as an act for a moment but as a journey, a process to advance, to improve continuously. This idea becomes impelling when you start with some issues easily put behind you early in the game.

At Panmunjom where the negotiations to end the Korean War took place, and in the Paris negotiations to end the Vietnam War, the parties each worked hard at blocking the other from proposing any easy preliminary progress. This is a play to achieve early domination of the negotiation. The shape of the conference table became a major issue. Agreement on an agenda might appear to be another form of easy step. When you hit roadblocks to defining even the simplest and easiest steps in the early stages, count on a long-drawn-out affair. Save your best cards until later on as you work through the easy items.

4. *Patience is needed to let the story unfold.* It may seem reasonable to be open and frank and expose all of your case early on with the hope that the other person will share your reasonableness. Don't count on it if serious issues divide you. Be slow in releasing your story. Fire off a few experimental rounds and see how they fly before you release the whole argument. Often the best part of the story comes last.

Two kids were seated beside a pond in the Deep South when two Yankee fishermen came along. It was a hot day and the fishermen decided to go for a swim. Approaching the youngsters, they asked, "Are there any snakes in this pond?" The kids shrugged. One of the fishermen reached in his pocket and fished out a nickel. "Here, kid, I'll pay you to tell us the truth." The kid sullenly took the nickel, and stated, "Nope, it's the truth, mister. There are no snakes in there." The two fishermen quickly doffed their clothes and splashed about happily for ten minutes. Upon returning to shore, one of the fishermen asked, "Kid, now be honest with me, why aren't there any snakes in there?" The kid looked at the nickel again. "Well, I guess the 'gators ate all of them."

Urgency has its moments, and the time to drive for a finish should produce energetic effort. On the other hand, when it's time to wait, urgency does nothing more than shift the advantage over to the other side.

5. *Spend as much time preparing as negotiating.* The authors, both long-time labor arbitrators, have seen again and again how often a good case has been watered down because one side or the other came ill-prepared to the session. Mediators report that similar experience is even more apparent in settling deadlocked bargaining. The highly paid but extremely busy lawyer who shows up at the session and dumps the contents of his briefcase upon the table, at which point he starts getting informed about the issues of the case, is setting his client up for a hefty loss.

During the sixties General Electric introduced a new technique of collective bargaining named for its architect, Lemuel Boulware. It was called "Boulware-ism." Its essence was that the firm would do extensive research all year long and be ready to present a package at bargaining which would be laid ont he table as a tidy package and then would stick in its heels. To the dismay of the Electrical Workers Union, who often were less well prepared, it proved to be a disastrously effective method. GE won bargain after bargain because of their preparation. The unions in turn began to develop greater preparation and better legal strategies and very costly strikes which cost the company hundreds of millions of dollars in sales and profits. Boulwareism ultimately had to be modified as the union also undertook better preparation.

6. *Avoid round-the-clock negotiations.* One of the favorite stereotypes of collective bargaining in labor relations is the marathon bargaining session. It runs night and day, the parties don't change clothes, shave, or eat proper meals. They occupy a smoke-filled room until the morning hours, break briefly for some refreshment and catnaps, and then back to the table. Such a practice may occur upon occasions when both parties are working under a deadline and neither wishes to quit. The quality of decisions under such conditions is sure to deteriorate, however, and while it may prove the durability of one side or another, it has few things to commend it as a strategy. It is when *fatigue* sets in that the essential concentration and attention needed to exploit bargaining advantages disappears. Judgment falters, memory blurs, and your resistance can lower. You are also doing a real axe job to your own physical health.

Closely related to the round-the-clock session is that which starts immediately after you have flown across eight time zones and your metabolic clock is about a full shift out of phase with the local time. Get there early enough to get rested. If you find yourself getting punchy, call a recess, and adjourn until you can get a full night's sleep. Avoid the jollity and entertainment which hosts will often urge upon you in a foreign land, and if the festivities are unavoidable, then add time for sleep before you start bargaining.

Suppose you can't avoid an all-nighter or a time-zone difference? Stick to some rules here:

a. Lay off the booze like poison. You are simply compounding the chance of giving away the whole farm.

b. Stay away from those intimate small dinners that go on until the wee hours, Have a token bite and turn in.

c. Monitor your own condition. If you look in the bathroom mirror and resemble a veteran of five days in infantry combat and smell like a slightly ripe goat, demand an adjournment. Go to bed until you are rested. Shower and return fresh and feisty.

d. If you can't break the session, try to have an alter ego or partner take over the lead bargaining job. If two of you are alternately carrying the mail, you might wear the other side down. You have to be sure the second bargainer is as well informed and competent as yourself. Before you turn the lead bargainer role over to another, caucus and get an agreement on what course to follow as a strategy.

e. Use some device to delay the bargaining when the pressure of time and fatigue get heavy upon you. One tactic used by a company president was to declare that his "health" wouldn't permit him to proceed without a recess and adjournment for eight hours. He then would reach into his pocket and take out a small bottle of pills (which were really sugar pills) and ask somebody, "Please, may I have a glass of water?" Laying his hand on his chest, he would often get the other side to rush to him with solicitous concern and *they* would ask for an adjournment. Placing his hand on his chest was often useful. Actually he had the constitution of a horse.

7. *When dealing from strength, open with a strong demand or offer.* This is the kidnapper game. You have snatched the infant son and the victim's father is a billionaire. Don't fiddle around with small talk. Just tell them how to make delivery of the million dollars. You must of course have a very strong position before you open the session with a strong, immediate, and very clear demand. Your final offer is your first offer.

A Wyoming rancher awoke one morning to find some heavy construction equipment on his property and a crew of people milling around putting on helmets, shoes, and jackets. With a rifle under his arm he strode out to the middle of the machinery and demanded to see the man in charge. The superintendent showed him a work order telling him to start excavation of a ditch across the rancher's land. Although the ditch had been creeping toward his property steadily for the past three weeks, it seemed that somehow the company had failed to negotiate the rights for this particular stretch of land. The rancher conspicuously cranked a live round of ammunition to the chamber of his rifle and announced, "Nobody has an contract to cross my land, and you better clear out now! You can drive your cars, but leave that equipment here. Then you can send your lawyer or somebody who really has the power to deal around here and we'll talk." Needless to say, the crew scattered promptly, and when the negotiator finally arrived late that day, he was presented with a clear, loud, and very expensive demand, which he meekly signed without a murmur. It was five times as much as others had received for the same rights.

On the other hand, don't try to lay out outlandish demands if you don't have the baby, the father isn't worth much money, and it isn't even his kid.

8. *Beware of surprises.* Failure to do your homework in anticipation of the opening of negotiations increases the chance of something surprising cropping just when things were going swimmingly.

An insurance claims agent was confronted with an aggressive husband whose wife had been injured in an accident, her car totaled. Rather than accepting what was really a quite generous settlement, he decided to go for something bigger and tripled the demand. The claims agent, not empowered to pay out that sum, called for a deferral of the discussion and went back and started checking for more information. He discovered that the woman's license to drive had lapsed by two days at the time the accident occurred, a fact hadn't known when he made the initial offer. He presented his new finding to the now humble husband, who promptly settled for considerably less than the original offer.

If you have such a skeleton in your closet, always be ready to deal with its being uncovered, and don't be surprised when it shows up in negotiation at the most inopportune moment. If you are convinced that it will be found out, it is better to freely divulge it up front and discount it. In one venture capital negotiation, the lawyer-promoter of a new firm had once been brought up on disbarment proceedings before a distant bar association. He had been vindicated, but was fearful that if it were uncovered tardily it could quash the whole deal. Thus when the capital provider got tough with him about "We of course will want lots of references, and the right to investigate you personally," the lawyer-negotiator-promoter calmly agreed. "I welcome such a full-dress investigation. You won't find a single mark against me, and you will undoubtedly discover the time I was brought up for disbarment proceedings in Nevada but was wholly acquitted. I will give you any details you wish on that case, including names and addresses and copies of the board's findings if you like." While it didn't add especially to his luster, it did avoid the surprise factor which could have chilled the potential investor.

9. *Press for an early concession.* Sometimes it's necessary to teach the other side in bargaining that concessions are part of negotiation. They don't learn this by watching you concede. This merely increases their appetite for more victories. The key part of this tactic is to obtain such a concession early, which gives you a reference point. It needn't be major. It often helps to find a simple error of fact in the other side's statements and have them concede that a technical correction is necessary. This will accomplish a worthwhile point if made early in the process.

Two department chairmen in a large university were debating the assignment of office space in a commonly shared building. One of them came on strong that his people would need "all twenty-one rooms" on the top floor. The other chairman quickly pointed out that there were only nineteen rooms on that floor and that two of the numbers were assigned to broom closets and utility space. "Surely you don't want to assign your faculty to closets and utility rooms, do you, Smith?" Smith smiled and quickly agreed that he had no such intention, at which time the other noted that he wasn't conceding any space on the top floor, but certainly appreciated the concession of factual error. It eased the climate considerably, for the original demand had been offered as "non-negotiable." The error of fact proved that indeed there was at least one negotiable feature, and that a concession had to be made.

10. *Check those deadlines.* One of the elements that helps produce the aura that surrounds a negotiation is the presence of deadlines. There seems to be something quite important about deadlines. They lend a sense of urgency, pressure to settle, and necessity to make concessions. Thus it is pretty important to assess how real the deadline is. Is it some kind of artificial goal which is being imposed to pressure you? The sales person who tells the customer "you'd better make a deposit on this property right now because I have another buyer looking at it at one p.m." is attempting to press for an immediate decision. If the property is desirable, and the acquisition vital, you may not choose to call his or her bluff. But if this property is merely the best you've seen thus far, you may call the bluff and look at other options. If the other options don't work out, you still can go back, and on many occasions will find that the property is still available, in which case you may reduce your offer below the original.

One salesman, deadlocked with a buyer, tried to undermine his opponent by threatening to go over his head to his boss. The buyer swiftly called his boss, made an immediate appointment, and sent the salesman into the boss's office. The boss, no novice at such things, informed the salesman: "Our time is valuable, and I will give you fifteen minutes to complete your business and be off our premises, or I will call a security guard and have you removed." The shocked salesmen went back to the original buyer and settled promptly. He had learned that you can face a genuine deadline.

11. *Sleep on a good offer.* That impulse to snap up a deal before it slips away has cost people more money, grief, and embarrassment than almost any other kind of negotiating decision. Even though the offer is

valid, apparently gold-plated, and worth taking, it is still advisable to suggest: "Let me sleep on it." Only an unreasonable adversary will press further, for there is an air of rationality about your suggestion that cannot be denied.

This is a wise adage in commercial and personal negotiations, whether it is horse trading or an offer of matrimony. Looking at the steed or the spouse the next morning may reveal attributes which were not apparent the evening before. A used-car dealer who won't let you keep the car for a day may be worried about what will fall off as it is parked in your driveway overnight.

12. *Silence can be influential.* An old short story tells of a goat and a lamb who met in the middle of a log bridge high over a swift-running river. The lamb made his first proposal: "Get out of my way. Jump over the side and let me pass!" The goat, making no sound, simply glared. "Well," the lamb proposed, "try standing aside so that I may pass by." The goat merely glared. The lamb then leaped off into the chasm.

There is an old saying also that it is better to keep your mouth shut and let people think you are a fool than to open it and remove all doubt. A dignified silence, coupled with a slow, steady stare and impassive manner, free of tics and manifestations of nervousness, are a useful, although not dominant, technique in some stages of the bargaining process. "In time I learned that my boss seldom disagreed or expressed anger at anything I said, but when he was opposed or very angry he was very, very silent," reported one manager. The boss in this case had taught other people well to read his moods. Such uses of silence are slow to impart and take time and patience to work but are an invaluable part of the skill needed in progressing the talks without slipping backward through a wrong phrase or statement.

13. *When you bluff, expect to be called.* It is sound strategy to count your chips before you bluff to see if you could afford the loss in the event your bluff is called. Mentally write off that amount, and figure out what your position would be after the loss is tallied. If it bankrupts you, better not bluff unless you have a plan for recovery from bankruptcy. As professors we have often advised young people to "get a savings account in reasonably liquid form which is equal to about a year's pay as soon as possible after you leave college and go to work. It will keep your bargaining position in the firm strong." The person at work who lives from one paycheck to the next is in no position to bluff, to issue ultimatums, or stick in their heels on some matters of principle. Having a comfort-

able savings account, or better still a rich spouse, a salable skill, a good job offer in your pocket, or even a very strong ego which can survive defeats without serious stress effects, makes your ability to bluff much more viable.

Bluffs usually work best late in the session when there is more to be lost on the part of the other side. They have made gains, earned concessions, and can see success in sight. The threat that it all may topple because of this single issue makes it more likely that the bluff will work.

14. *Use recesses and caucuses.* A young engineer who had a fractional ownership in a product patent which was the firm's main revenue producer had a serious disagreement with management. They suggested that he sell out and go off on his own. They needed his product and wanted to clear him out of the business where his disputes were troublesome. The owners were older, experienced executives, and he was quite intimidated by them, and by the prospect of negotiating. He had no idea whether he should settle, and if so on what terms. At the suggestion of a former professor, he took his wife to the sessions. At first the management was indignant, but he calmly explained that "as my heir she is an interested party to this negotiation." They reluctantly bought that. The wife as it turned out provided a very valuable contributor to his negotiating performance. Whenever he got angry or flustered, or the other side got domineering, she quietly suggested a caucus. She and her husband would then retreat to the local restaurant for a cup of coffee where they relaxed, talked about the kids, and agreed on a strategy to use when they returned to the room. Throughout two days of very intense bargaining, when each major point came up she kept calling for a caucus. It got to a point where all parties would look immediately to her to see if she was going to call a caucus. The settlement ultimately proved very satisfactory to all, and the management of the firm suggested in the wrapup, "Mrs. X, if you ever want to take a job in management in this firm, please call us." The caucus is a valuable breather and space provider, inserting paragraphs of time into a negotiation that might otherwise be going awry. It is in fact the principle tool of time management for negotiators.

Recesses perform an equally valuable function. Ask for a recess of a day, a week, or a month to study the situation and come back. The negotiations are not dead because they are spaced out in time, but the timing of them is one of the strategic tools of the skilled negotiator.

15. *Expect stalemates and deadlocks.* A deadlock happens when an immovable barrier is assailed by an irresistible force. Nothing seems to

give. You see no possible solution and it seems that agreement will never come. If you remain deadlocked, the parties in fact may be locked pathologically into their positions. The substance of the issue is no longer as important as the principle of winning. There are three rules for coping with deadlock:

a. Recognize the deadlock and try to overcome it by power and force first, to see if the other person really is as intractable over time as they appear at first.

b. If deadlock is persistent and apparently can't be broken, caucus and identify the goal once again clearly. Then find a means of *going around* the obstacle rather than continuing to beat your head against it. (You could always give in, but that may not be necessary.)

c. Find some means of collaboration if one is possible. Two people are working in a library. One wants some fresh air and opens the window a few inches. This causes a draft which irritates the other. He goes to the window and slams it shut. The other quickly goes back and opens it wider than before. The other goes to the window and slams it and locks it. This could go on forever or could accelerate into open warfare.

"I see that you are warm and want the room to be cooler. On the other hand, I dislike drafts, which could affect my health and blow my papers around. May I suggest that we open a window in the next room and open the door between? You would then get some cool air and I wouldn't be annoyed by the draft. Don't you agree that this would solve both our problems?"

The key here is to identify the real basis of the deadlock and avoid fixation into a pathological deadlock, in which winning for its own sake is symbolically more important than the substance of the needs and wants of each.

16. *Beware of late hits and nibbling.* Herb Cohen, the noted author on negotiation describes nibbling as what occurs when a customer tries on forty different suits before choosing one. The sales person by this time is completely frustrated and is willing to settle on anything. That's when you ask, "What kind of tie do you plan to throw in on this deal?"

A farmer entered into lengthy negotiations with a government agency which wanted to use a segment of his property for a highway alteration. After more than a week of interminable dispute, the farmer finally gave in and the agreement was struck. The bulldozers and graders would start the next day. The government team was jubilant. To take him to court to win their rights might delay the project until spring. Just as the farmer had the pen in hand to sign the agreement, the officials watching breathlessly, he stopped, turned calmly to the boss of the other side, and added, "By the way, I have always wanted a little pond for my cattle in that corner of the property, which would be easy for your equipment." The official quickly gave in to the nibble. "How deep?" he asked. Nibbles often come when the other side is frazzled, close to a deadline, or simply defeated and tired.

You can avoid nibbles against you by summarizing with such statements as "and that's it, isn't it?" or "let me summarize the deal." Nibbles always are a matter of timing and only work well at the end of negotiation, when the other person thinks he has won, the papers are ready, and the thing is finally done. To nibble too often on each issue as the negotiations go along could prove irritating and heighten the resolve of the other party to nibble back on the succeeding issues.

17. *Recognize subtle changes in trends.* In one session the customer kept insisting that full service costs would be paid for by the seller. Things dragged along and at the end of the third day of negotiation, during a caucus, one member of the selling team pointed out a new trend in the discussion. "I have noticed that not once today did he mention those service costs which he mentioned ten times on Monday." Often the things that are not said are evidence of a trend toward softening and should be watched as carefully as the things which were said openly. Demands which have been increasing in intensity suddenly become stable. If you demand something, listen carefully to the response, for it may be as important if the other person *didn't say no* as if he said a quick yes. In one heated negotiation about annual job objectives between a president and vice president, the consequences were important, for the goals being determined would be used at the end of the year for bonus calculations. The vice president reported later:

"I knew I was on the road to a major win when the old man stopped turning his back to me when he talked. During the early hours he was practically always with his back to me, talking either to the wall behind him or over his shoulder at me. As I began laying more facts on him, and giving him some new concessions to think about, his swivel chair began to inch around until at the end he actually had his elbows on his desk and was facing me, and I knew we were in agreement."

The important thing about trends during negotiation is to keep in mind that negotiation is a process, not an event. It is a time-phased string of occurrences which produce agreement. Notice the pace of negotiations. Are things speeding up or slowing down? Are the side tracks increasing or decreasing? Is the other side introducing more or fewer extraneous issues? Have they caucused more or less? Does it seem that they are calling somebody back-of-the-scenes more often, or moving ahead and calling their own plays more or less? All of these trends can be indicators of progress and guides to response.

In a subsequent chapter we'll examine more fully what the wider social trends in negotiation are. Here, it's sufficient to note that as part of your time management, you should watch *pacing* trends.

18. *Recognize when agreement is close.* In lengthy negotiations it often seems that they will go on forever. Positions get stuck, arguments become routine and tiresome, and it is easy to overlook progress however subtle. Having a member of your team watch such progress, perhaps keeping a progress chart, may help you read the signals that agreement is imminent. This is the time when the pace can and will pick up. The settlement of small bargaining-chip issues will fall quickly into place, and the big issues move to the fore for settlement. This is the time when top figures are apt to reenter the field and start to make the final decisions.

"At first the president of the company and the vice president of the union started the bargaining. But as it dragged on, the pressure of other business took them away, and the small technical issues were left to subordinate managers. Then one day, all of a sudden both of the top people appeared, they started some horse trading, and we all knew that the final agreement was near." Thus reported a labor relations manager for a large firm in the Midwest. Knowing when such a point arrives often signals you to make rapid changes to reach a settlement, rather than hanging onto strategic positions for future advantage. When the deal is ripe to be made, make it!

19. *Don't push too far. There is a breaking point.* An executive lost a valuable briefcase with personal effects and credit cards in an airplane VIP lounge. He received a phone call (collect) from a youthful caller. The negotiations went like this:

"I have found your briefcase and papers."

"Thanks a million. I appreciate your honesty. Would you please send it COD to this address?"

"Are you offering a reward?"

"Well, yes, twenty-five dollars for your trouble."

"That is not enough."

"Fifty dollars?"

"Way too low."

"What do you want?"

"One thousand dollars!"

"Keep the case, it and the contents are insured."

The caller had pushed too far.

20. *When the mission is accomplished, tie it up and leave.* Poker players know the futility of turning over the next card in the deck after they have folded. Don't stick around after the agreement is wrapped up for postmortems. It is often possible to sour the relationship by confessing that you would have paid more, or that your price really was much lower. Don't try to gloat or win verbal and psychological victories after the agreement is complete. Once you have the agreement signed and sealed, pick up your copy, shake hands, smile, and depart. Avoid any personal recriminations, estimates of the other side's abilities, or tales of what might have been.

The result of the agreement in negotiation should be confirmed in writing except in the most exceptional cases. Talk-first-then-write is a safe guide to most negotiations. In goal setting with the boss, one of the parties should confirm the agreement with a written memo which doesn't add or subtract from the agreement. Each has a copy for reference to rate actual performance during the period ahead.

Reversing your actions can be embarrassing. A young man who planned to join the Army was given a farewell party at work including some generous gifts and a hero's departure. He flunked the physical exam and went back to work. What can he do with the gifts? Likewise, quitting shouldn't be done without a firm bridge to cross after the departure. It is not easy to have to go back and confess second thoughts.

21. *Manage the length of the agreement.* During the fifties many firms triumphantly made a great break with tradition in collective bargaining by negotiating five-year contracts. This was supposed to produce a half-decade of industrial peace. In some cases it worked exactly the way they wished it would. In others, times changed, and product improvements and cost reduction programs made five-year contracts undesirable. Before you negotiate the term of an agreement, that is, when will it begin and end, be sure you have some kind of reason for choosing that period. As an experienced policeman told his rookie partner, "You will stay alive longer if you make it a rule never, never to go through a door until you are pretty sure you know what is on the other side."

Westinghouse got itself trapped in some long-term contracts for supplying atomic fuels during the seventies and later found them very costly. In the plastics industry in 1973 many a firm ran a cropper when they found that their long-term contracts with customers weren't matched by long-term contracts with the suppliers of raw materials. The materials, it appeared, were petroleum-based and the Arabs suddenly jacked up the price of petroleum by 400 percent. This left the plastic companies with contracts to deliver at a low price, but a requirement to buy the raw materials at a radically higher price. They went broke in large numbers. Each contract might have been competently negotiated, yet the whipsawing between the two long-term and short-term agreements left them up a creek without the proverbial paddle. A restaurant may want to lock up a prime space lease for many years to exploit its advantages for some time to come. But if the location sours, they still have the long stretch to live out their ill-timed agreement. Such matters require considerable research and a certain amount of crystal ball gazing before you deal.

22. *Set a time limit in your offers.* A large utility let a construction and repair project out for bids. Unfortunately they were not specific about the closing time for bids. Three firms came in with their bids, which were opened. Three days later a fourth firm came around the corner with a lower bid and demanded the contract. A close study showed that the wording of the closing time limit didn't specify whether the bid should be in the mail on that date or received at the office. Further, the date fell on a weekend with a Monday holiday. The utility opened the bids on Friday night. On Tuesday morning the fourth firm came forth with their bid and a strong statement that since the bid specified the weekend date which was not a business day, this automatically carried the bid date over until Tuesday. The officers of the other firms strongly suspected that some quiet leaking had occurred over the weekend. The original three bidders threatened suit if the contract was awarded to the fourth. The fourth threatened to go to court if their bid was not accepted as the lowest bid.

In negotiations it is sometimes fruitful to set arbitrary time limits for agreement on a point or clause, thus threatening to open what seems to be an easily resolved issue to further prolonged haggling. "We are now ready to make a proposal which will be open for firm acceptance in the next fifteen minutes. After that it is closed and we shall reconsider it." While this may be meaningless in some cases, in others it may turn the tide of indecision and waffling into a hard answer.

23. *Counterpunching is often better than striking first.* There is often

more clout in the potential of a blow which is yet to come than in actually swinging out first. The withheld action has elements of anxiety and doubt which can add weight to its real force. The ticket scalper has his greatest clout before the game starts. The good negotiator doesn't always put forth his best shots at first unless he has little or nothing else to do. If your ideas have given out, it may be tactically a last resort to whack at the opposition, shout at them, and pound the table with a shoe as Nikita Khrushchev did at the United Nations. If on the other hand you have some good ideas as weapons, firing your heaviest and most unpleasant rounds early could mistakenly indicate that you have run out of ideas.

THE MANAGEMENT TIMING

Lots of management conferences these days deal with time management. This perfectly useful stuff improves your efficiency. In the drawn-out process of negotiations, however, time management refers to the importance of timing. The weight of the argument can be enhanced by delivering it at precisely the moment that it will have maximum impact. This requires practice and skill.

PART III
OVERALL MANAGEMENT OF YOUR NEGOTIATION EFFORT

In the following chapters we'll look at the management process in negotiation. Should you negotiate through a team, or should it be done by one skilled individual acting alone? What is the role of top management in your negotiation strategy? How do you train your people to be better negotiators? That's the topic of the following chapters.

12
Organizing Your Team for Negotiations

Many hands make light work.
—John Heywood (1560)

In the fall of 1970 the United Automobile Workers struck against General Motors despite numerous previous statements from both sides that they did not wish to strike. Further, the Secretary of Labor, President Nixon, and other peak union leaders all expressed a strong hope that no strike would occur. The company employed 800,000 workers directly and millions of others in supplier firms. Yet the strike was called. Was this simply a break-down in the meeting room where negotiations were being held? To assume such would be a gross simplification of the negotiation process in this industry. The union on the one hand was being pressed by its members whose wages were being sorely taxed by inflation. The company, as President James Roche told the St. Louis Chamber of Commerce in February 1970, was faced with inflation which had eroded profits, and he said the union was mainly to blame. Cost increases were not being recovered through price increases or improved productivity. The union also wanted a strong cost-of-living clause which would index wages more closely to inflation; and further, a provision for early retirement after thirty years of service was demanded by the employees confronted with the monotony, drudgery, and meaninglessness of factory life. Clearly the breakdown in negotiations which occurred was a product of considerable behind-the-scenes pressure from those who weren't present at the bargaining sessions. The strike, which lasted until November 20, was finally called off by the membership by an overwhelming margin, but only after a loss of millions of dollars in profits, the depletion of savings of the workers, and devastating losses to surrounding communities in tax income and to small businesses dependent upon income from General Motors workers.

The strike and subsequent settlement demonstrated the complex behind-the-scenes level of organization and communication which important negotiations can demand. A study of these negotiations and hundreds of others shows clearly that the management of team negotiations is as important as the actual behavior of skilled bargainers in the meeting room itself. Tricky verbal ploys and Machiavellian gambits in offer and counteroffer won't affect the outcome if the people behind the scenes have important needs and wants which they expect their negotiating team to fulfill. While most negotiations won't be as broad in scope or as important in economic outcome as the General Motors negotiations with the UAW, there nonetheless remains a great residue of principle which should govern team effort in negotiations. That is the subject of this chapter. The following list of seventeen team management methods will help you do a better job of preparing for team negotiations which can lead to agreement.

1. *Choose the team leader early.* As soon as the date for negotiation has been fixed, select the individual who will be responsible for managing the negotiations. Such a person should probably not be the top executive of the firm, but rather one who is skilled in negotiation, has the confidence of the top management, and has experience in the organization and a knowledge of past practices, past negotiations, and prior agreements. This person will then assume individual accountability for the preparation, planning, selection, and management of the team, collection of data, and actual operation of the bargaining sessions. Among the important early steps is the choice of the alternate leader in the event that the first should be removed from the scene by illness or other reasons.

A small Midwestern newspaper found itself unionized, and to conduct the actual bargaining it employed at the last moment a labor lawyer with a reputation for aggressive, hard-nosed bargaining. In order to save legal fees, the newspaper reduced the time he might spend in advance preparation and briefing about the company, its problems, its history, its people, and its needs and wants. Unarmed with such information, the lawyer adopted a hostile and aggressive stance, but made numerous errors in statements of fact, and within a short time had provoked the first strike against the firm. Subsequent attempts by the union to reopen negotiation were rejected, thus producing several charges of unfair labor practices, considerable unfavorable publicity, and ultimately the near bankruptcy of the company. It wasn't until the lawyer was replaced in negotiation with a senior editor with wide knowledge of the company and the employees that a settlement was ultimately reached. Even then, the new chief of the bargaining team was handicapped seriously by the damage done to relationships by the first negotiator's lack of knowledge and truculent style. Choosing an insider with strong negotiating skills, perhaps even some training in formal negotiation, and backed by a behind-the-scenes authority figure upon whom he or she can call for counsel, authority, and assistance, will enhance the negotiating power of the chief of party.

2. *Organize your information well in advance.* The chief of the negotiating team should be empowered to go wherever necessary to obtain all of the information needed to conduct aggressive negotiating. This means assured access to accounting, marketing, personnel, and other statistics, and a budget to acquire such information commensurate with the importance of the outcome of negotiations. Other members of the bargaining team should be chosen for their ability to dig out such information and perhaps attend the negotiation sessions, in order to clarify meanings and interpret facts for the spokesperson during negotiation.

3. *Construct a portfolio of needs and wants for your own side.* These are the four squares explained in Chap. 4. Four categories of information should be sought out and identified:

a. Those items which you both need and want. These are your top objectives in negotiation.

b. Those items which you need but don't necessarily want. You might for example need to hold prices at a fixed level, but would have to give up certain management prerogatives in control of the work force to get them.

c. Those items you don't really need but would like to obtain. These will be your bargaining chips.

d. Those items which you neither need nor want very badly. These might be labeled your "walk away" items.

These lists of four classes of demands and objectives must be severely restricted in exposure, for they would comprise a valuable packet of information for the other side. They should be divulged only on a "need to know" basis, and then only in partial form except to the chief negotiator and his or her alternate, as well as the top management of the firm. It is about this portfolio that communication with top management should be most complete by the head negotiator.

4. *Construct a portfolio of the other side's needs and wants.* Matching your own needs and wants, you should attempt by several means to estimate the needs and wants of the other side. This can be assigned to a

member or two of the bargaining team who have considerable knowledge of the other side, what they have said and done, what they have released to the press, what can be deduced from conversations with members of their organization, and skilled estimates based upon placing yourself in the other person's shoes. Some organizations use what is called "pub research" to achieve this information; that is, they send people into nearby bars and places frequented by the other side in the forthcoming negotiations. Also, talking to the other side's customers, vendors, bankers, and community associations can often produce useful information in constructing their portfolio. Pay due regard to the fact that the other side may be doing likewise.

Just as the skilled coach in athletics will have certain members of his team don the uniform of next week's opponent and scrimmage the first team, it is helpful to use such a portfolio in simulated or mock negotiation in advance to see how they will develop in action. Some firms use special reports from sales persons who call on a customer to report conditions which have been picked up in the course of selling. Purchasing agents similarly can pick up useful information from calling salesmen about the target firm. Brief notes reporting such information may be invaluable in estimating what the other side will be asking for, where their sticking point will be, and where to give in quickly.

The dean of a college in a large university was preparing in advance for budget negotiations with the administration. Through personal conversations, some discussions with members of the budget chief's staff, written policy documents, and memos issued over the past year, he was able to gather that the chancellor, who was the chief decision maker on budgets, was most interested in innovative programs, rather than mere administrative neatness on the part of the respective colleges. Accordingly the dean entered budget negotiations with descriptions of several exciting new programs which called for larger funding. This helped him win out over other schools which pleaded for more funds based upon vague and lofty statements such as "Our scholarly efforts will be erased without further increases in funding."

The *driving force* behind the other side's negotiation efforts will be those matters which have the highest levels of *need and want.*

5. *Assemble all important factual data into organized form.* Making members of the preparatory team put all of their collected research into systematic form, probably notebooks with clear indices and topical headings, will ease negotiation and make the data more accessible when it is needed in bargaining.

The commercial development department of one national firm requires a notebook for each major area of bargaining for mergers. Each notebook is prepared by a staff member of the bargaining team in advance. It is reviewed in team meetings in which the preparer of the research makes a full presentation of his findings. Questions are asked, and further digging may be prescribed. When the pre-negotiations briefings are complete, the entire team is aware of the overall picture, and the chief spokesman is solidly grounded in all aspects of all of the issues. These notebooks are brought to the sessions and are immediately available to be studied and referred to by the team member in charge of that area. Such areas as these were included in merger negotiations, each with its own notebook:

Profit history of both firms
Assets growth
Personnel and human resources profiles
Compensations structures
Product lines
Market shares
Stock price history
Legal suits past and present
10-K forms for the past five years
Annual reports
Credit reports

6. *Organize and train the negotiating team.* The chief of negotiation is usually the spokesperson for his or her side, although this may not always be true. In some instances it is the alternate. Another person should be the recorder, and bringing a secretary to record the sessions and issue summary statements as understandings are reached is sensible, and in important or high-dollar sessions, essential. Keeping the actual number of people on the team to a few major areas of expertise is better than bringing in everyone who has been involved in preparation. If they have done their preparation work well and the documentation is complete, it remains for the negotiators to carry the case for your side forward. Role playing is an effective method of training your team in some pre-bargaining sessions. If some of the major issues are anticipated, it will pay off handsomely for your side.

A major department of government which has enjoyed considerable success in budget hearings before Congress has developed a finely tuned team of insiders who role play the other side. Comprised of people who can simulate Congressional questioning with considerable accuracy, the team going up to the Hill finds itself ready for the toughest questions that can be thrown at it.

7. *Manage your experts carefully.* Never call experts to testify in your behalf unless you have complete confidence that you know what they will say, and further, how they will respond to tough questions. This can be achieved by paying them extra for days of briefing, questioning, and simulated cross examination. Be sure their credentials are impeccable and there are no secrets about them which if divulged during negotiation would damage your side.

8. *Spell out the rules of speaking.* Inexperienced members of a bargaining team who see an apparent opening for a clever, wise, witty, or telling remark can often set negotiations back a long way unless they are restrained by the rules of speaking. In one bargaining session between the city administration and the police union the issue being debated was the rights of the commander to specify uniforms for officers on duty. The management side wished to retain command authority over the police force. The police union, on the other hand, was concerned about safety and health. The patrolmen were irked over orders to wear summer uniforms until October first, which often led to chills and colds for officers on late shifts when the weather in late September turned cold. The chief, on the other hand, was concerned at the reluctance of officers to wear protective clothings such as bullet-proof vests in dangerous situations. In the midst of the argument, one younger officer broke in to suggest, "We can stand rocks and bullets better than we can stand goose bumps, chief." A dead silence fell over the negotiation. It proved the chief's case that many officers were reluctant to wear the protective equipment when ordered, and exposed a disrespect for orders to wear protective gear, and the union was forced to give in. If the young officer had been restrained, the union might have won the right to request warmer clothing when needed. It was not about to try to defend the reckless and heroic posture of the younger Turks against personal protective gear, and thus lost both.

Private conversations, short caucuses, and passed notes and memos should be used to communicate with the spokesperson during negotiation, and all other communication quashed unless the parties are asked to speak by the spokesman.

9. *Use committees for subtopics in negotiations.* Members of the bargaining groups may be appointed to subcommittees to complete details

and flesh out the exact wording, costs, and details of general agreements. This saves the time of the main negotiators, makes progress faster, and trains members of the team for possible roles as chief negotiator in future bargaining. Such assignments should have specific objectives, and appointees should not be granted general powers of agreement. "It is agreed that the general level of hospital insurance costs shall be no more than $1.50 per hour to the company. A subcommittee is hereby appointed to define the details of that coverage, and other details shall be included under this price agreement. The committee shall report within two days after consultation with representatives of the insurer, the benefits manager, and the insurance manager of the union." This gives them some latitude for detailed items to be covered, and requires some reference to experts, but limits their decision powers.

In one large firm where general managers of divisions met annually with executive vice presidents for divisional goal setting for the coming year, often the division manager's controller was assigned to meet the corporate controller to work out details of product mix to maximize profits for the coming year. Each agreed in advance that the product mix determined by the two subordinates—in effect a subcommittee—would be the objectives of the division manager for the coming year.

In selected cases, the committees should include people who are not present for most of the negotiation, but serve on an ad hoc basis to report their findings to the main session, and then to depart.

10. *Establish and monitor communications.* It is a responsibility of the team leader to establish a plan for communication during the negotiation. In union relations, information passed to management and in some companies down to the foreman level about progress in negotiation will have some beneficial effects for the firm. While wide open communication can have some chilling effects upon negotiation, it is useful to issue periodic reports on progress, problems, and issues as long as such communiques don't echo back into the bargaining sessions and alter them or destroy them. Communications include the following:

- Keep top management fully informed about as much detail as is necessary to assure that agreements will be backed by them. State the issues, main arguments, and recommendations.
- Keep all members of the bargaining team fully informed about changes in policy, direction, tactics, or strategies which have been decided by top management.

- Delegate certain study or research projects to members of the team. Give them complete instructions, including limitations and constraints upon their actions.
- Define with the other side rules for communication with the press and the public at large. Generally it is sensible to obtain agreement that no public statements will be issued by either side unless agreed to by both sides. Ordinarily it should be considered an evidence of a breakdown of negotiation if either side goes to the press with its story without the consent and agreement of the other side.
- Maintain tight security over your side's information, data, memoranda, notebooks, notes, and records. You may be handing the other side a distinct advantage if you are careless with such mundane things.
- Obtain briefings from outside the sessions about any comments, facts, opinions, rumors, or data floating around in the firm, the community, or the press about the negotiations, and discuss with your team the implications of such reports for bargaining progress. Changes in the other side's personnel, position, or attitudes should be included in such intelligence. In one large firm, several months after the negotiation was completed and the company had been forced to give up several tough concessions, it was discovered that a young lawyer on the bargaining team was married to a secretary for the other firm. Without any intent to do wrong, dinner-table talk about the negotiation occasionally ended up in the hands of the other side, thus arming them with information about a weakness in the company position. In addition to developing your own information sources, be sure your own side has no leaks, however inadvertent. Ask members of your team directly if they have any personal off-job connections which could possibly be used to obtain information about your side's position. If such a knothole exists, better eliminate such a person from presence at negotiation, and especially from caucuses and inside information. Not only should members of the team be checked, but secretarial persons typing papers, and employees in the duplicating room where copies are prepared should likewise be monitored.

11. *Define a suitable time schedule.* In some instances negotiation is conducted nonstop and pursued to exhaustion or settlement. In other cases there is a persuasive reason to spread the negotiation over time.

If you have reasons for delay, then space the negotiation out as much as possible. If you have pressing needs for settlement, then strive to have them spaced out in shorter intervals. Define your own time pressures and seek to space the timing of negotiations to fit.

In one large city's public library the chief librarian professed to favor "participative management" and scheduled regular meetings with staff members to discuss objectives, problems, and practices in operation of the library. At one session the librarians expressed a strong desire to discuss working hours for the staff, which the chief did not wish to make a subject of discussion. Accordingly he proposed that they hold a series of discussions on that subject over the next three months in monthly meetings. The librarians, noting that the busiest part of the year would be past by the time discussions were completed, urged a more immediate schedule, which he denied. At the end of three months when no progress had been made on the discussion of hours, a union organizer had been seen talking to the librarians in the circulation departments. The chief immediately moved up the meetings for the future into a "one-day conference" the following week, and an amicable agreement was worked out quickly.

12. *Selecting members of the team.* There are five ways people tend to get on negotiating teams. (1) They are appointed by a higher-level person. (2) They are recommended or chosen by members of the team presently aboard for their abilities, knowledge, responsibility, skills, or interests. (3) They are elected by membership on board of directors, formally or informally. (4) They volunteer. (5) They are ex-officio or selected by their position. Certain people will be automatically part of the negotiating team because of their office or rank. However they are picked, the job should be made attractive to them by the team leader. Being a member of the team should be seen as an attractive assignment because it meets personal needs, has enhanced status, will be interesting and exciting, will be developmental, will afford some challenging experiences, may gain benefits for their own department, or provides an association with important people whose opinions and high regard they value.

On the other hand, members of the team should be apprised of what is expected of them in terms of time demands, hours displaced, personal sacrifices and inconveniences, incursions into personal time, pressures and work loads, and interruptions of ordinary work routines. The standards of performance for team membership should be spelled out personally in face-to-face discussions, and confirmed in writing. If they work at middle or lower levels in the organization and team membership is in addition to their regular work, their boss should be apprised of the requirements of the assignment as well, with follow-up reports on performance which can be noted in their performance reviews. A good briefing for new committee members should:

- State the team objectives, including its authority to act.
- Locate the team in the organization structure.
- Define the size of the committee plus its support research staff if any.
- Name the contact person in charge to whom communication should be addressed, and from whom information will be received.
- Provide a schedule of meetings for pre-negotiation sessions.
- State the estimated times and places of negotiation sessions.
- Describe fully and firmly all security procedures.
- Define the decision procedures, including voting or consensual procedures to be employed.

13. *Deciding the number of members.* The ideal committee size according to behavioral science research is five members. (Bales 1960). This of course is a generalization which must be varied as the need arises. Most of the research which produced this ideal number was based upon factors internal to the committee functioning, and external factors may dictate more or fewer members. This ideal size may be tempered by some of the following factors which affect the size of the team.

- The cost of larger committees is high, both in the direct expenses of their housing and travel and in the time lost from their regular duties.
- The role of each person is clearer when the group is at five. Over seven members tends to produce some dead weight and redundancy and increases the likelihood of conflict, error, or wasted time in explaining, training, and the like.
- Having an odd number rather than an even number reduces the likelihood of deadlocks within the team over issues being discussed, such as alternative strategies and tactics.

- Groups of three generate problems of an overpowerful majority. Almost inevitably, two will dominate one by a coalition.
- Four-person groups increase the likelihood of antagonism and disagreement.
- Where the leader has control, the span of control is better managed in five-person groups than larger ones. The organization of the negotiating team should not follow a division of labor as would occur in a large group such as a football team with offensive and defensive coaches having autonomy over their group. Negotiation teams should function more like a basketball team clustering around the coach as a father or older-brother figure with authority.

14. *A negotiating team calls for a leader who is directive and task-oriented in his behavior.* Unlike other kinds of leadership which may be present in the organization, when the time for negotiation comes, the directive leader will do a better job. When there is a task to be performed, being a leader with high control gets you rated better by members of the group in accomplishing the task. (Schlesinger 1969) Weak leaders in fact will bring forth a lot of take-charge kinds of action from other members of the group and can lead to conflict and ambiguity in the team. While leadership sharing and acting as a "facilitator" has a place in many situations, it is not likely to work best in the negotiating committee. This task achievement job includes such actions as obtaining information, initiating ideas, evaluating, answering questions, and giving opinions.

One of the reasons for this strong leadership role is that the negotiating team is often a temporary organization, and studies have shown that an organization put together for a specific purpose works better under directive leadership than under a more participative style. At the same time as he is directive and task-oriented, the leader should have a high level of consideration for members of the team, and those leaders who are high in both consideration and concern for results will come off best. (Blake 1962)

15. *High levels of cooperation are better than conflict.* If the negotiating team is divided among itself, it will achieve less satisfactory results than if they have high levels of cooperation. It is practically impossible to keep behind-the-scenes conflicts from emerging in the bargaining room. Thus the leader has a major responsibility for resolving inter-

group conflicts and producing unity on the team before entering the bargaining room. Studies show that when people get along, hold each other in high regard, and have been motivated to cooperate rather than compete, they will be more effective than groups comprised of people trying to outshine one another in the sessions. (Hare 1960). Friendliness, intergroup cooperation, mutual assistance, avoidance of jurisdictional disputes, and willingness to be attentive to others' ideas are important elements in this collaborative effort. People with similar personalities, backgrounds, values, and attitudes toward the company, and who are predisposed to accept others on the team at full value, make for better team performance and fewer disagreements between subgroups and factions. The leader in such instances is better able to mold the group into a team than in cases where unlike people are patched together to negotiate. The leader can often produce this unity of effort by personal persuasion and support of members rather than by force and orders. Thus the strong controlling leader combines tasks and personal influences to take charge of negotiations.

16. *Decision making inside the negotiating team.* The best form of decision making inside the negotiating team is one which is consensual rather than democratic or dictatorial. The leader in such a format will thus listen to all opinions, show understanding of all positions, but retain the power of final decision, which is announced after all sides have been discussed. Taking votes leads to splits and lack of unity among the team. Dictatorial order giving by the leader, even when he has the power, can lead to costly mistakes in that the valuable contributions of some members may be overlooked or ignored.

17. *Keep your top authority out of the actual sessions.* There is one role which is of sufficient importance that it deserves a separate chapter: that of the chief executive officer. This may be the president in some cases, or the general manager of the division in another. In lower levels it may be the plant manager or the department chief. Usually this person stays out of the actual bargaining and remains in the background removed from the heat and fury of the give-and-take negotiating, but is constantly informed of the issues and arguments, and intervenes when it has the maximum bargaining impact. Let's look at that in the next chapter.

Before doing so, however, you may wish to check your own team organization practices for negotiations against the 17 points listed in this chapter. Rate yourself on a scale of 1–5 with 5 highest.

1. Do you choose the team leader early enough? —
2. Do you organize your information well in advance? —
3. Do you construct a portfolio of needs and wants? —
4. Do you construct a portfolio of needs and wants for the other side? —
5. Are all facts organized into readily usable form? —
6. Do you organize and train the negotiating team? —
7. Have you spelled out rules for speaking? —
8. Do you have subcommittees for subtopics? —
9. Do you establish and monitor communications? —
10. Can you manage your experts carefully? —
11. Have you defined a suitable timetable? —
12. Has selection of team members been done carefully? —
13. Have you chosen the right number of members? —
14. Is the leader directive and task-oriented? —
15. Do you have a plan for cooperative team membership? —
16. Is your decision-making style proper? —
17. Do you keep the top person out of the sessions? —

Total —

On any items in which you rated yourself under 3, go back and review the text once more. If you rated less than 65, restudy your whole team-building process. Over 75 means you probably have a sound team plan for negotiation.

13
The Role of Top Management in Negotiations

> The only way to make a man
> trustworthy is to trust him.
> —Henry L. Stimson

The president of a medium-sized manufacturing firm believes in giving individual managers free rein in handling intercompany negotiations. "They're the best judge of their operating needs and strengths," he explains. "Give them the responsibility and they'll produce." Accordingly, when a contract with a major customer comes up, the sales manager is given full authority to conduct the negotiations. Although highly motivated, the manager lacks the knowledge to speak for, much less integrate, the different needs and priorities of other parts of the company that are also affected by the negotiated terms of the agreement. Because he knows his own department best, he ends up maximizing its interests and commits the firm to a five-year contract that severely strains both production and finance. Company profits fall.

The president of a retail company is proud of the reputation she earned as a negotiator during the building years of her business. Whenever her firm is engaged in negotiations, she monitors them closely and often intercedes in the talks at the first sign of difficulty. Her authority, she feels, can help expedite decisions and cut through all that unnecessary muddle. However, as her company has grown in size and complexity over the years, she has become less knowledgeable about the specifics of her products. Executive responsibilities limit the depth of her preparation. The quick settlements that she achieves are often lopsided—in favor of the other party.

This chapter by Jeb Brooks and Earl Brooks originally appeared in *MSU Business Topics,* Summer 1979, and is reproduced by permission of the authors.

Neither of these approaches to managing negotiations is unusual in American business today. Both, unfortunately, are ineffective. Top management participation is critical to successful negotiating, yet too few presidents understand the role they must play. On the one hand, the high stakes involved in intercompany negotiations demand the concentrated involvement of top management; on the other, it is a complex and time-consuming activity which requires judicious delegation of responsibility and authority.

What little has been written about negotiations is concerned with tactics and the actual process between parties. Scant attention has been directed toward understanding the chief executive officer's point of view. This article speaks to this gap. We begin with a brief overview of the role, then focus in depth on a practical analytic framework for the chief executive to use in planning objectives, guiding preparation, monitoring progress, and assessing results. While the degree of the CEO's direct involvement depends on the type and magnitude of the particular negotiating situation, he or she must provide direction for all negotiations. The costs of ignoring this role can be high.

Robert L. Katz has pointed out that in successively higher levels of management, two abilities become increasingly important: (1) coordinating all the activities and interests of the organization toward a common goal (conceptual skill), and (2) understanding and motivating individuals across departments (intergroup skill).[1] Nowhere is competence in these two skills more important than in managing the negotiating process.

The flow chart set out in Figure 1 traces both the conceptual and intergroup responsibilities of the CEO from the preplanning stage to the final point of assessment and evaluation. The specific actions called for fluctuate between (1) the CEO being directly involved with the negotiating team and the other party, and (2) the CEO taking a back seat, delegating responsibilities, and playing supportive and coordinating roles.

The flow chart includes set points at which the chief executive officer can check that the long-term welfare of the total organization is being considered. However, as perhaps the only person in the company who holds and can speak for this perspective, the CEO is responsible for maintaining this overview role throughout the negotiating process.

Preplanning. Top management should decide, often after considering staff recommendations, what operational objectives may best be real-

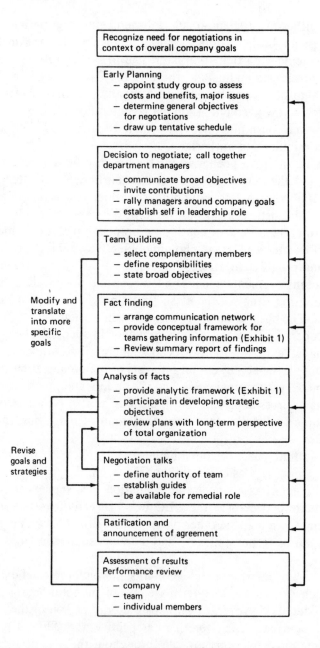

Figure 1. FLOW CHART—THE ROLE OF TOP MANAGEMENT IN NEGOTIATIONS

ized through negotiations. For example, the policy decision by the president of a sporting goods company to concentrate on the development of highest profit areas led to a task committee's recommendations to sell off the fledgling company equipment operation and to acquire a sailboat manufacturer to round off the small boat line. Both proposals called for intercompany negotiations.

At this point the negotiating process starts. The chief executive's first step involves directing the task committee or a separate study group to prepare a preliminary report on the costs and benefits of negotiations, the issues likely to be involved, and the companies that might be approached. This information enables the chief executive to undertake the second step: to draw up a tentative schedule regarding planning, preparation, and the duration of the negotiating talks.

Too often negotiating teams face a single-choice situation because management did not plan enough lead time. The more alternatives open to a company, the greater is its power in negotiations. Whenever possible, the chief executive must allow sufficient time to explore, develop, and use options. Time is needed not only for in-depth preparation and analysis of issues but also to enable public and private sources of information to be tapped early. It is far easier to learn the other party's pricing and decision-making processes six months before the negotiations than it is on the eve of the session.

This initial information gathering should be expanded prior to actual negotiations.

Rallying the company behind a common goal. As mentioned above, the chief executive officer is responsible for viewing the company as a whole and recognizing interrelationships, that is, how various functions depend on one another and how a change in one part has consequences for all others. The CEO must also think in terms of relative emphases and priorities and must strike a balance among conflicting needs and values of departments. (In fact, negotiations occur continuously within every organization—from vice presidents vying for capital budget funds to a salesperson arguing with a credit manager over what terms to offer a customer. However, intracompany negotiations are not within our scope and will be discussed only as they relate to negotiations with outside companies.) In the face of change—such as accompanies intercompany negotiations—intracompany competition is heightened. Top management must pay special attention to this conflict and try to direct it into a constructive mode.

Soon after deciding to proceed with negotiations, the chief executive should meet with concerned department managers to discuss their needs, views, and preferences. The CEO must not commit himself or herself to specific plans, but rather should agree to explore options. This early participation can foster a cooperative sense among department managers so they all feel their specific values have validity; it can help ensure that each department know there have to be trade-offs and compromises in negotiations but that decisions to advance the overall welfare of the organization will benefit everyone. The CEO must clearly convey the message that he or she will assume responsibility for making those tough decisions.

These preliminary meetings serve a purpose beyond motivating and gaining the commitment of personnel holding different views. They pave the way for subsequent fact-finding efforts. In effect, the chief executive has given authority to the negotiating team in the eyes of individual department managers. Opening these channels of communication is essential for the planning and preparation that must go into the negotiations.

Building the team. In large companies, the chief executive generally lacks (1) detailed current knowledge about products, technologies, and customer needs, (2) the necessary patience or time to prepare in depth for and engage in the actual negotiations, and (3) the specific skills required at the bargaining table. For these reasons the CEO must concentrate on broad strategic issues and rely on a team of skilled negotiators. This team will work with members of the organization to develop background information, goals, strategies, and tactics, and then conduct the negotiations. [See Chap. 12]

Most negotiating teams include a leader who organizes and speaks for the group, supporting specialists to provide technical assistance, experts to bolster credibility, and a note-taker to record what is said—and not said—during the negotiating sessions. Management must judge the situation the company faces and select team members accordingly. (If dealing with a monopolistic seller, management might select a persuasive negotiator with an encyclopedic capacity for facts and figures. If the firm itself is the sole seller, a negotiator of high status and low tolerance might be most effective.)

While there is a tendency for chief executives to pick members in their own image—hard-nosed bargainers to mirror their own tough-mindedness, or technical people if they themselves are engineers—

research indicates that an effective negotiator has a combination of traits: competitiveness and cooperation; skepticism in perception and positiveness in presentation; ability to speak and listen well; and good business sense and a practical understanding of human nature. Because such individuals are rare, management often builds a team with members who complement one another. A large retail company has had outstanding success pairing a "dumb questioner" with a sharp cost accountant at the negotiating table. Respectful but persistent, the questioner needs to understand thoroughly most assumptions the opposing party considers as given. Needless to say, he and the accountant work well together.

Management also must know when to bring in outside consultants for the team. During the 1950s, a drug company began negotiations with government officials to build a plant in Latin America. Their central approach was to stress the financial advantages of their proposed project. Fortunately, management included on the team a consultant familiar with Latin American operations who pointed out that decision makers in this particular country placed far greater weight on political than on economic considerations. The company revised its approach and now enjoys successful operations throughout Latin America.

The importance of this comprehensive analysis cannot be overemphasized; company negotiators must have a facility with the issues that allows them to understand and deal with the varied combinations the other party may present. In addition, the analysis of issues will help the team prepare its own alternative strategies and package proposals.

The chief executive must instruct the team to preserve flexibility. The negotiating process is dialectical: What one part does depends on the moves and countermoves of the other. An unexpected concession by one side may allow the other to change a nonnegotiable demand. Options must remain open. Although issues and priorities may change, they must always be understood.

Taking risks. Few business opportunities can be known with certainty; instead, they present themselves in terms of relative tendencies and probabilities. This is especially true with negotiations. (If terms were known in advance, there would be nothing to negotiate.) Reducing uncertainty can reduce risk. The knowledge gained from the planning and preparation processes discussed here should lessen uncertainty for the negotiating team.

There are two additional actions the chief executive can take to encourage risk-taking by the team. First, state that he or she understands and accepts the risks of planned strategies and objectives. Commitment to high goals also increases the likelihood of stalemate. Every part of the organization, including the board of directors, if appropriate, must be prepared for the implications of deadlock. Second, the CEO can give team members a general assurance that they are regarded as competent professionals who will not be second-guessed at every turn.

The role of top management with respect to tactics. The CEO helps develop strategic objectives and priorities but leaves tactics, for the most part, to the discretion of the negotiating team.[2] Certain tactics, however, such as the use of publicity or the take-it-or-leave-it gambit, should not be used without management's approval. Also, the chief executive officer is responsible for the ethical and legal standards of those representing the company and must never condone lying, deliberate misrepresentation, or illegal acts. A policy based on presentable facts will best serve the interests of the company.

Management should assure itself that tactics used by the team are in the company's long-run interests. Squeeze tactics used in a one-shot deal with a real estate agent, for example, would be inappropriate for negotiating the latest contract with the union. However, in some situations this distinction is not so clear.

In investment projects in Third World countries, the balance of power often shifts over the course of the project.[3] When terms are negotiated at the entry stage, the investing company has the relative power. But as the host country begins to gain knowledge (perhaps as expectations prove unrealistic or new investors accept less attractive terms), the power balance changes. At this point, the host government may insist on renegotiating the terms of the original agreement, disrupting company operations.

Top management, with the aid of its broad perspective, might foresee this danger and consider providing officials of the host country with more information in an effort to make their expectations more realistic and to reduce the area of future dispute. Although such action initially would result in less favorable investment terms, the long-term prospects of the project would be enhanced.

Final preparation. As seen in Exhibit 1, the dry run and drawing up the agenda for negotiations are the final steps in the preparation. Management should direct team members to hold practice sessions to pool and assess all they have learned and to anticipate how the negotiations

Exhibit 1. Checklist for Gathering and Analyzing Information

Your Company

Assess product and service need

- break down into components
  - characteristics of product and service
  - time requirement
- determine relative flexibility and alternatives for meeting need

Project worth of their product and service to you

Assess department capabilities

- needs
- strengths
- limitations

Determine major issues

External factors

- trends
- condition of market
- economic, government, and social context

Other Party

Assess their product and service need

- break down into components
- determine their flexibility and options

Project worth of your product and service to them

Evaluate company

- organizational structure
  - decision-making process
  - authority of their negotiators
- general business and financial conditions
- history
  - performance record
  - description of prior negotiations

Project their major issues

Project negotiating position

- strengths and limitations
  - time
  - knowledge
  - resources
- brainstorm to determine their likely demands, strategies, tactics, questions and answers

Determine

- relative position and power
- opportunities for cooperative problem solving
- trouble areas

Set goals — Refine broad objectives into specific goals

- categorize as essential, desirable, tradeable
- for each issue prepare
  - high target
  - an acceptable minimum
  - starting price
  - reason for that starting price

Develop primary strategy and alternatives

Develop tactics

Prepare support data for
- internal company use
- presentation to other party

Suggest agenda for negotiation talks

Conduct dry runs

Prepare questions to test assumption and estimates

The Negotiations

are likely to unfold. Drawing up the agenda—that is, outlining what issues need resolving and the order and timing of those decisions—presents an opportunity to gain control of the talks. It is clearly advantageous for the team to suggest an agenda.

Finally, the CEO should caution the team not to assume too much. Research is an invaluable aid in preparing for negotiations, but misjudgments can be costly. Early in the session, the team should plan to ask questions to test its assumptions and estimates.

THE NEGOTIATING TALKS

If the planning and preparation have been done well, the actual negotiations should go smoothly. The chief executive officer rarely will be directly involved in the talks and, in fact, must refrain from trespassing. Interference can cause serious damage to the credibility and sense of authority of the team in the eyes of the other party.

This is not to suggest that top management should never sit at the bargaining table. Its presence may be necessary in certain situations, such as (1) initial meetings, to display interest and commitment, (2) to speed decisions or break deadlocks, and (3) to arrive at an agreement in principle (the legendary Onassis handshake), with details to be worked out by respective staff.

Related to this topic is the decision the CEO must make about how much authority to delegate to the team. Restraint is essential. Full authority is often a great handicap—history is filled with blunders made at summit meetings—whereas limited authority gives the negotiator additional time to think and plan countermoves while checking upstairs for approval. Also, with limited authority, negotiators can give budget limitations, company policy, and an adamant boss as reasons for not making a concession. (During the acquisition heyday of the 1960s, a major conglomerate often used a representative of relatively low status to make the initial approach to the president of the target company. In the event the feeler was refused outright, this tactic left room for a high-level executive to follow up with a sweetened offer.)

Generally, a negotiator who has easy access to decision makers and who can obtain quick and decisive responses will not lose credibility or power.

Occasionally, a representative of the other party may go over the head of the team and attempt to deal directly with top management.

This can set an unfortunate precedent. A few years ago the president of a large trucking firm permitted the traffic vice president of an automotive company to circumvent his negotiating team and deal directly with him. Not only was the morale of the president's team damaged, but also this action established a pattern in future negotiations for leapfrogging at the first sign of difficulty.

Once the negotiations begin, the CEO should be available to play a mediative role. The other party may spring a surprise, such as a sudden change in demands, authority, deadlines, or negotiations. The team should be instructed never to respond to such situations until it is prepared. In the event additional information needs to be gathered and new goals and strategies developed, the role of top management with respect to the team proceeds as in the earlier preparation.

The CEO has other responsibilities. He or she should arrange to be informed of significant progress in the talks and, to the extent other departments of the organization are affected by different negotiated packages, should make certain that they are kept informed of developments. However, as mentioned above, the CEO must resist monitoring progress too closely. By their nature, bargaining sessions are confidential, and the frequent reporting of tentative agreements or lack of progress can cause leaks harmful to the delicate negotiating process.

In addition, the chief executive is responsible for all decisions to introduce extra resources, to make changes in the negotiating team, or to discontinue the talks.

Ratification. When the parties are moving toward agreement, provision usually is made for periodic noting of progress. In the Paris fashion industry, for example, there is a wire around the negotiating room on which daily summaries of tentative agreements are posted. Successful negotiators can sense a willingness to settle. Often, at this stage, a private meeting of one member of each party is held to reach an understanding, the details of which are filled in by representatives of the two teams, subject to further refinement by legal and other staff groups. These drafts are then submitted to the top management of each side for approval. If ratification is not forthcoming from one party and additional concessions are requested, the other CEO should consider carefully the ramifications of granting additional demands.

Generally, top management should not be afraid to ratify a contract that is in substantial agreement with the company's goals. If an important issue remains unresolved, a statement to this effect should be included in the final agreement. The act of ratification may serve as impetus to work out the additional compromise.

Often, ratification is simply a formality. If the chief executive officer has received periodic reports over the course of the negotiations, there should be no surprises in the final agreement. Once a careful study has been made to assure that the contract is a complete and accurate representation of the terms agreed upon during the session, the executive may commit the company to implementing the agreement.

Assessment and performance review. The CEO is responsible for appraising the results of the negotiations in light of performance objectives. The framework presented in Exhibit 1 provides essential points of reference. Within each area—from planning and preparation to the actual sessions—the CEO should evaluate successes and errors and look for ways to improve negotiating performance in the future.

This evaluation should include an assessment of the team and its individual members. Although negotiating tactics may be a technical skill not everyone can master, managing the negotiation process, including understanding how negotiations can be used to meet needs and create opportunities, is an ability that managers need to learn and develop. The CEO should make certain that negotiating skills are included in the management development program of the company.

Conclusion. In summary, the role of the chief executive officer in negotiations is a complex one that demands many executive skills. The CEO's responsibilities include providing the necessary overview and conceptual framework, organizing staff and team, helping plan and make decisions regarding priorities and objectives, and motivating negotiators to achieve them.

There are no simple solutions in negotiations; there are only intelligent choices. It is the responsibility of the CEO to provide the framework and direction to help accomplish the company's objectives.

14
Head to Head—Negotiating on Your Own

> The more ignorant a man is, the more
> he is inclined to separate his private
> interest from the interest of his fellows.
> —Jeremy Bentham

Some of the most important negotiations you will engage in won't involve a well-organized team of supporters and researchers, but will be done by yourself. If there is any pre-negotiation study done, you must do it, and if any research is entailed, you must do it yourself. Not only are you alone in such bargaining, but the outcomes will have greater possibilities of loss or gain than when you are a member of a team. It's true that if you fail to represent your employer competently you can hardly expect to get any medals, but often the personal losses are minimal. After all, bargaining in teams backed by a decision maker in the wings gives you some built-in alibis for failure. When you go head-to-head with another party, however, your failure to negotiate skillfully is your own responsibility. What are some of the cases in which you must negotiate as an individual, not as a team member?

- You are constantly transacting business inside the house with bosses, subordinates, other departments, people on the same level, and service departments. You might find that you are maker and seller of services inside the organization, and the users of your service may dicker with you about the time, cost, quality, quantity, and continuity of those services.
- Purchasing agents report that much of the negotiating they do is with users inside their own firm who use a variety of ploys to circumvent and thwart company procedure. Users' departments may encourage salesmen from outside to engage in back-door selling,

going around purchasing to go directly to engineering. Other users place rush requirements upon their requisitions which aren't always necessary, giving you less than normal lead times to make up for their own procrastination. Users sometimes contact vendors for product or service specs before they contact purchasing. A few place orders directly, then come to purchasing with a confirming invoice to be paid. Others are late in returning answers to queries, making it necessary for the purchasing department to place rush orders or to expedite in a hurry. Users sometimes fail to let purchasing know about vendor failures. Still other users become emotionally attached to a particular vendor and insist upon sole-source buying. Engineers and technical people often want to gold plate the material, calling for high-cost overdesign by the vendor with no real functional gain. All of these call for some in-house negotiations between purchasing department and end user. Purchasers also must negotiate with their own employees, with top management about budgets, and with their superior about purchasing department objectives.

- Personnel managers must negotiate with many others in addition to the union. Inside the house they must deal with general managers to gain acceptance of personnel programs. They must negotiate with superiors over objectives, with divisions about personnel practices to be implemented, with bosses about budgets, and with managers about salary increases for their people.

- Production managers must deal with production planners and schedule makers about schedules. They must deal with engineering about tools and fixtures, with maintenance about availability of equipment for repairs and overhaul, with employees about grievances, and with quality control departments over shipments held up. They must bargain over standard costs with the cost accountant, with industrial engineers about work standards, with purchasing about materials, with shipping about packaging and delivery dates, and they must define objectives with employees and foremen. Finally they must sit down with their superior and negotiate objectives for the coming year or quarter.

Without trying to be exhaustive, it's apparent that every position in the firm has extensive occasions when the success or failure of the department is being determined by the outcome of bargaining, transacting, and negotiation. The American Association of Industrial Management in Philadelphia has proposed twelve tips which will get these face-to-face negotiations off on the right foot through the use of persuasion:

- Win the respect of the other side. They must respect your word and your actions.
- Avoid arrogance. The know-it-all has a self-imposed handicap, generates resentment, and builds resistance to what should be an easily sold idea.
- Don't shut out the other side. Listen to every criticism and proposal in an objective fashion. If they are correct, thank them, and if not, rebut them calmly. If you get caught, ask for help.
- Pick the right time. Your best idea may be lost if it's rushed, too late, or catches the other person at the wrong time.
- Don't oversell. Never claim more for your case than can be delivered and never say that something is a fact when it isn't.
- Use a positive rather than a negative approach. Be affirmative and hopeful rather than negative and destructive. Rather than attacking the other side or its motives, show the features and benefits of your own case.
- Don't apologize. Stress the positive features of your case. Don't engage in apologetic or derogatory comments about your own case.
- Avoid being a pitchman. Sergeant Bilko is quickly recognized, and often isn't trusted. Don't try to be too slick. Sincerity is the most effective persuader.
- Be well prepared. Don't get surprised by something that shows up during the negotiation or you will be left second best.
- Anticipate their questions. Answer them in your original story before they are presented, if possible.
- Anticipate their objections. Here again, try to overcome their objections by anticipating them, and answering them in your affirmative statement of your case before they are presented.
- Keep your cool. If you are angry, don't show it; call a caucus, and don't let resistance to your ideas provoke a hasty angry retort.

All of these of course are somewhat repetitive of what you've read in prior chapters of this book, but there are a few modern techniques from the behavioral sciences which can help you be more effective in negotiation.

USE THE PRINCIPLES OF TRANSACTIONAL ANALYSIS

One of the more interesting and valuable of the new tools of behavioral sciences to emerge in the past twenty years has been that of Transactional Analysis (TA). It was developed first by Eric Berne, a California psychiatrist, to manage face-to-face transactions. The human personality, Bryne suggests, can be divided into three distinctive ego states:

Parental: This is the part of our personality which we acquired from our parents and parental figures. Things which our parents said to us are retained throughout our lives and when triggered by life situations will come forth as overt behavior in our relationships with people. If our grandfather or father was judgmental ("You rotten little kid"), we are apt to respond thus to somebody else sometime in the future. If the parent figure was nurturing ("How can I help you?"), we likewise may use this approach when our parental state is aroused.

Adult: This is the mature, reflective, problem-solving part of us. It is orderly, rational, and conscious and is usually a product of past learning acquired during our growing up.

Child: This is a most interesting aspect of our ego state. All of us, Berne suggests, retain elements of our childhood in our personality, and when that facet is triggered we revert back to early child behavior. One part of this stored behavior is *natural* childish behavior. This is our emotional, creative, delighted self. More often, this ego state causes us to pull out of our unconscious memories our *dependent* child condition ("Why is everyone always picking on me?")

These three states, which are oversimplified somewhat here, show up in transactions such as an individual negotiation session. We may at one moment act parental, at others, adult, and at still others we let our child state emerge.

Furthermore, the other side has the same three states. This means that even when only two people are in the process of negotiation there are *six* ego states in operation, and this provides us with a useful way of handling negotiations.

Thus it isn't simply *us versus them,* or *you versus him/her.* Rather it is one of your ego states confronting one of their ego states. This means

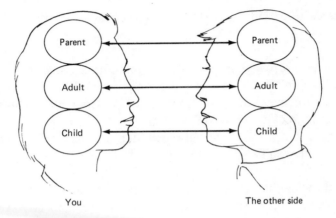

Figure 14-1. How Ego States Look in Face-to-Face Negotiations.

that any of the following combinations of transactions could be going on at any moment in negotiation:

Parent-Parent: These are two judgmental people clucking over something mutually concerning them. "Isn't it awful the way inflation is killing the market?" "Yes, I don't know what will happen next."

Adult-Adult: These are two negotiators acting like rational, orderly, civilized persons. "Do you have a price list for these special items?" "I am sorry, I don't, but I will obtain one for you and have it here by tomorrow."

Child-Child: This is the delighted sharing of immature egos, or mutual conservation. "The boss is always picking on me." "Me too, let's throw a brick through his window."

If you study these and create some behavior examples of your own, you will be able to recognize the ego state the other side is adopting, as well as recognizing your own.

In addition to the existence of these states, Berne points out, it is possible that people will attempt to *play games* with the other side by manipulating the other person's ego state to win an advantage. This leads to a fourth kind of transaction, the *crossed transaction*. Such a case exists when you start a negotiation in an adult state and the other side adopts a parental response. You then are tempted to become childlike.

a. "May I borrow your typewriter, Jim, mine is broken?" (Adult)
b. "Why don't you take care of your equipment? Do you think I am going to cover you every time you get in trouble because of your infernal recklessness?" (Parental)
c. "Oh, you can take your old typewriter and stick it. I'll find somebody who isn't so picky and critical." (Child)

While all of this has an amusing and interesting air, it can be deadly serious, for the other side may deliberately attempt to hook you into your child state while holding only the parental state themselves. This gives them a kind of game advantage.

After you have mastered the three ego states and recognize the various combinations, start using it in negotiations. Here are a few rules you might find useful in applying TA in your negotiation:

1. In opening the session a little small talk of a parent-parent nature, discussing the weather, the world, politics, and the like may put you both at ease and on an equal level.

2. In certain cases you may even engage in some child-child level discussion for openers. Describing something funny, or showing and telling something that will appeal to their lighter side, can establish equality at a lower level. Talking about something humorous, or being clubby, often is a child-child condition. Old friends going back many years may actually evoke old school ties and the like. This is okay for openers.

3. Adult-adult discussion is the ideal mode for negotiation, with only occasional diversions into the other states. "Let's get down to business, Jim."

4. Many of the ploys, gambits, and Machiavellian tactics of negotiation are those of the wily, defensive, and dependent child. In many other cases they are designed to intimidate the other side and force them into a childlike condition, making them dependent, defensive, and angry. People who attempt to dominate others in negotiation through the use of power are often acting out a parent-child transaction.

5. When confronted with any state other than the adult, your best tactic is to *retain your adult condition* at all times and by whatever means possible. Listen carefully. Restate their argument or verbal

assault. Describe in an adult fashion that you understand their words and can see their feelings clearly. When the other person behaves in a child fashion, don't become parental, but act adult. If they scream, pound the table, walk about or even walk out, keep your own ego state orderly, rational, and conscious and deal with the problem accordingly.

The lesson of transactional analysis for negotiators is in the importance of the adult ego state being retained at all times. If you must become parental, make it the part of the nurturing, helping, and coaching parent, not the judgmental and critical parent.

The following statements were actually overheard in negotiation sessions. In the blank spaces to the right, indicate whether the statement is Parent (P), Adult (A), or Child (C).

1. "The trouble with your proposal is that it is careless, inaccurate, and filled with nonsense." ___

2. "Nobody talks to me like that." ___

3. "Perhaps we should go over those numbers one more time just to be sure we are in agreement." ___

4. "That was a pretty rotten thing to say to me, why are you so hostile and aggressive all the time with me?" ___

5. "I'll pull your hair out, I'll claw your eyes out, you insufferable beast." ___

6. "Isn't it awful about interest rates? I can remember that in 1937 the prime rate was 1.5%." ___

7. "If you would care to go away and study your facts and figures more carefully, we would be open to another meeting after you have done your homework properly." ___

8. "Anybody can make a mistake. Haven't you ever made one?" ___

Anwers: 1, P. 2, P. 3, A. 4, C. 5, C. 6, P. 7, P. 8, C.

Figure 14-2. Test Your Ability to Apply TA to Negotiation

If you missed more than three, go back over the text again and study the three ego states. Make up some statements of your own.

USING A PROBLEM-SOLVING APPROACH IN NEGOTIATION

Experienced negotiators will recognize the term "looping back on itself" as a common hitch which delays negotiation. This looping back occurs when people fail to define the problem they are working on with care and intelligence. Let's look at an example:

The state commissioner of education was asked to approve, as required by law, the request by a superintendent of a large school system for six days during the school year when selected teachers would be freed from classroom duties to engage in special instructional improvement work. Under the superintendent's plan, any teacher so chosen would be allowed up to six days a year to engage in special studies which would improve curriculum, to meet with parents, train paraprofessionals, or develop special teaching techniques or materials. The local school board endorsed the idea and agreed to provide the funds for substitute teachers for such time off and small amounts for extra materials and supplies.

The response from the commissioner's office was immediate and emphatic. The plan was flatly refused. The justification was that state law required that all pupils be given 180 days of classroom instruction yearly, and no exceptions could be made.

The superintendent, exasperated at the commissioner's apparent lack of understanding of the plan, requested an appointment to discuss the proposal. The commissioner refused to even make an appointment. "After all, the law is clear and no exceptions can be made, therefore I see no point in meeting." Over the next two years this dispute opened again and again, and each time the superintendent sought to meet and explain the real facts, his request was denied. After three such refusals, the original request had been replaced by the new issue: "Why won't the commissioner even meet with me to discuss the case?" The commissioner, notably irritated, stated the case as being "Why doesn't the superintendent as an intelligent man realize that it is pointless to even discuss the question of my approving an illegal action to release students on the school's part?" A symbolic issue had become paramount. The symbolic dispute was one of "To meet or not to meet." The argument from that point forward turned around the desirability of meeting. Arguments about responsibilities and powers, delegation, legalities, and authority of the commissioner about having a meeting occupied everyone, including several lawyers. Finally the school board produced a court order, and the commissioner was forced to attend a meeting with the air decidedly cold and adversarial.

When the superintendent explained that the substitute teacher provision would legalize the teachers' having time away from their regular classes, the commissioner finally eased up. "I didn't realize that they were going to hire substitute teachers when the regular teachers were away. If they had thought of that in the beginning, I would have approved it right away."

What was going on all during the period when the debate about having a meeting at all was being fought out was the process of looping. *Looping* occurs when two sides look at two different problems under the impression that they are both looking at the same problem. It is a variety of the barroom argument in which two people who are actually in agreement appear to be in dispute.

"I tell you that Babe Ruth was the best baseball player of all time."

"You are all wet. Red Grange was the finest running back ever to don a football uniform."

"I say it was Babe Ruth" (referring of course to baseball).

"Baloney, it was Red Grange" (meaning of course football).

"You are an awful fool" (a symbolic generalization).

"Your mother was the village idiot" (reply to the symbolic argument). As the looped argument continues, it grows on itself and no agreement will come because the issue hasn't been clearly defined.

How can this be resolved? This can be shown in Fig. 14-3. The problem?

1. Define the present situation and seek agreement on the facts of the situation. Keep reiterating facts until both are in agreement as to the issue. (A)

2. Identify the ideal objective outcome for both parties. (B)

3. Look for alternative ways of arriving at a unity of method which would solve the problem for both sides. (C)

First you define all the facts of the case. Next you define the objectives of the parties. Finally you reach an agreement on what the problem (the issues) might be.

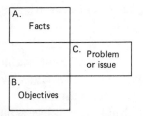

Figure 14-3. A Problem-Solving Model for Defining Issues.

Presuming now that we have sobered up our debating pair to a point where some rationality might be introduced, the issue can be defined as follows:

Facts: Babe Ruth was a super baseball player, and probably the best ever according to one view, which is not disputed. Red Grange was the greatest running back in football in the opinion of the second party, a view which is not disputed by the other side.

Objective: The purpose here is to choose two classes of athletics and select the greatest player ever in each of them. The objective then is to *name two persons in two fields.*

The issue: Is Ruth the greatest in baseball and Grange the greatest in football in the considered (not to say sober) view of the parties?

This model for problem solving has numerous advantages. It starts with the most verifiable area of discussion, the assertion and verification of the facts. Facts should not be confused with bias, with causes, nor with solutions, and should be backed by evidence.

- It requires that each side define its own objectives and that those objectives be stated in explicit terms.
- This means that a problem is a "deviation from an ideal or objective." If there is no deviation, there is no problem and therefore no issue. The parties are agreed.
- The problem is solved when the facts and the objectives are congruent or the same.

Take the case of the husband who has commuted for twenty years to suburbia, and each day on the way home stops and imbibes six martinis before arriving at his abode. Upon arrival, his spouse immediately starts to berate him about his drunken condition. He thus continues to drink to ease the pain of her nagging, and she nags even harder to get him to stop drinking. What is the issue?

Fact: He drinks. She nags. They do so simultaneously.

Objective: A happy marriage.

The issue: There really isn't any. Each is a neurotic whose most pressing need in marriage is to have a complete justification for their own personal pathological behavior. They have a symbiotic relationship, for who else would stay married to a drunk but a nag, and who would stay married to a nag but a drunk? Each has a built-in rationalization for what to some observers seems to be neurotic or abnormal behavior. Conclusion? They have a marriage which for the moment meets the needs of each.

Oh no! you may protest. I have different objectives for marriage. It should be stable, sober, loving, and supportive, like yours and mine. You have thus imposed your objectives upon this happy pair, and created for them a false issue. If perchance they should miraculously decide to adopt your objective, then the issue would change to something like "How to stop her nagging and his drinking." For the nonce, however, we shall leave this blissful pair to their mutually agreeable relationship.

The point of course isn't domestic felicity but defining issues. Using the problem-solving approach with the other side will get you to problem definition and issue resolution faster and avoid looping into symbolic terms.

The difficulty in defining the issue to be negotiated lies often in the conversion of the facts and individual goals of the two sides into a symbolic issue. While they may be seriously divided over the symbolic issue, they may find unity of agreement over the issue with some discussion of the objectives of the other side. The decline from facts and objectives to symbols to pathological separation is a rapid path which occurs all too often in the early states of negotiation and bars early progress.

NEGOTIATING WITH YOUR BOSS

One of the crucial kinds of negotiations most of us face is dealing with a boss over our responsibilities, what our job objectives are, and what standards will be used to measure our performance.

The system of management known as Management by Objectives has numerous commendable features when it comes to such negotiation. In brief, this system has been defined as

A process whereby the superior and subordinate managers of an organization jointly identify its common goals, define each individual's major areas of responsibility in terms of results expected, and use these measures as guides for operating the department and assessing the contribution of each of its members.

The distinctive feature of this system, which is used by some 80 percent of the Fortune 500 list of largest corporations, and by over 50 percent of the hospitals with over 300 beds, and is an official system of management in numerous government agencies at federal, state, and local levels, lies in the requirement that the boss and subordinate negotiate those goals. In order for such a system to operate effectively, each must prepare in advance with some study and decision making about their mutual expectations of one another. There are, however, some distinct differences between the way each defines his expectations of the job.

1. *The boss defines the purposes of the job* in terms of results expected, outputs hoped for, and constraints in areas of cost, quality, service, and time.

2. *The subordinate is charged with choosing the means* by which these objectives will be attained, within constraints of policy and law.

As Orville Beal, former president of the Prudential insurance company, once defined the relationship, "Purposes flow down and methods flow up."

Thus the negotiations provide that each side has a distinctive role to play, a responsibility to accept, and an accountability to the other. The superior must be aware of overall corporate goals, the strategic guides for getting there, the resources available, and the methods and timing of measurement of results. The subordinate has accountability for achieving those results by taking necessary actions to achieve them, by changing behavior to produce the results, and by exercising due diligence and care in faithful fulfillment of commitments made at the beginning of the period for which the goals apply.

If you are the superior in such a situation, you must avoid defining both goals and detailed methods, but confine yourself to establishing end results in specific and perhaps measurable terms, seeking agreement about the level and quality of those results.

Here is how the boss should conduct himself in negotiating goals with a subordinate.

A results-centered negotiation is a planned private discussion which periodically answers . . .

these questions	in terms of
1. What is expected?	Objectives
2. How are we doing?	Results (quantity, quality, service, cost)
3. How can we improve results?	Planned action
4. Why is it important to improve?	Motivation

Who	What	Why	When
Between each employee and the person he reports to.	To cover: Objectives, current performance on present job; results, accomplishments, and opportunities for improvement	To recognize progress; to develop mutual understanding and commitment; to plan for even more effective performance—by the individual and the group.	As often as needed; at least annually with quarterly follow-ups.

Providing continuous commitment and involvement in

- Providing the leadership and stimulating the ambition to reach for demanding objectives.
- Communicating to every employee how his contribution relates to these objectives, and importantly, how he will share in results.
- Providing initiative and motivation for the future with a positive attitude toward improvement.

Figure 14-4. Getting Improved Results Through Planned Discussions and Commitment

GETTING READY—YOU AND YOUR SUBORDINATES

1. As the first step in getting ready for results-centered management (MBO) it is necessary that you and each of your subordinates agree upon what is expected in terms of results. For each position there should be a statement of the conditions which exist when satisfactory performance has been attained in:

   a. Regular duties
   b. Management innovation and development
   c. Improved relationships
   d. Speed of response

2. This statement of objectives should be developed jointly by the supervisor and the incumbent and should:

   a. Fix accountability and responsibility in writing.
   b. Set attainable objectives expressed in terms of quantity, quality, service, expense, and time.
   c. Cover significant factors which really matter and are within the control of the incumbent.

  d. Enable measurement by the incumbent and by the supervisor.
  e. Establish priorities and dates.
  f. Be used continuously in communication of what is expected, what is being accomplished in terms of results, and how improvement can be attained.

3. Using this statement of objectives, ask your subordinates to prepare for the discussion by thinking through the results they are now getting, a few areas in which they could improve, and what they feel you as supervisor could do, refrain from doing, or do differently which will help improve their results.

4. A week or so in advance, schedule a time and place that will be convenient, private, and comfortable for the actual performance review. Allow plenty of time for the discussion and avoid interruptions.

5. Think through in objective terms what you expect of him or her in their present job. What results do you expect in each of the areas for which he or she is responsible? What measures do you both have to determine how well he or she is doing? Review the person's job responsibilities, indicators of performance, objectives, situation statements, action plans, and related operating records.

6. What results is this person getting? How is he or she doing in each area of responsibility? Make notes of specific examples for discussion of accomplishments and areas for improvement.

7. Think through what you are doing to help your subordinate improve performance. What more can you do in delegation, communications, coaching, facilities, stimulation, and recognition? What are you doing that impairs his performance?

8. Determine what needs to be said during the discussion: the opening, the most effective approaches, the possible reactions (yours and theirs). Tailor your approach to the person and the situation. Get ready to listen with interest and understanding.

DISCUSSION OF PERFORMANCE

1. Let the person know that you consider this discussion important. Be sincere, natural, and businesslike. You might wish to start by asking what questions exist concerning duties, responsibilities, authority, or organizational relationships.

2. Seek understanding of yourself, the person, your mutual relation-

ship, objectives, goals, and responsibilities. Consider accomplishments, problems, and opportunities for improvement. What *results* are being obtained? Save discussion of promotion and potential for another time.

3. Listen attentively. Encourage your subordinate to talk and to ask questions. Make the person's current performance the central subject. It would be helpful to find the areas in which he or she has made significant improvement in the past year, and his or her plans for improvement in regular duties, innovation, development, and relationships.

4. Ask him or her to discuss four or five areas selected for improvement during the next year. Discuss plans to improve on each. Later, ask how he thinks you can help him improve. When you both agree on what can and should be done, make notes of the plans, goals, and objectives for your later use along with duties for follow-up.

5. Ask what you as the supervisor could do, refrain from doing, or do differently which would help him or her do an even better job.

6. Discuss your impressions of performance in each responsibility. Start with those where improvement is needed. End with those on which he or she is doing an outstanding job. Use examples. Concentrate on a few areas for improvement. Avoid the "fine, but ..." or "however" technique. Also avoid the "sandwich technique"—a "good," then a "bad" and a "good."

7. Avoid using the terms "weaknesses," "faults," and "shortcomings." Stress areas for improvement.

8. Concentrate on results and actions rather than personality traits and peculiarities.

9. Especially avoid dwelling on isolated incidents or mistakes of bygone years.

10. Compare each person's performance with the standards for their present job. In your discussion do not compare one person with another.

11. Keep open-minded. Be willing to change your viewpoint or even the way you do things. Try to understand others and your working relationships with them.

12. Be careful in giving advice. Encourage each person to work out specific plans for improvement.

13. Be cautious in making promises. Keep the ones you make.

14. Review the points agreed upon. Be sure that notes are made of the important points, particularly action plans for improvement, objectives, and targets. The supervisor and the incumbent make their own notes, with each of you having a copy for follow-up. End the discussion on an encouraging note of confidence for improvement.

ACTION FOLLOW-UP

1. Capitalize on your performance reviews by putting into effect the agreed-upon plans for improvement, and regularly following up on action plans. Replan when necessary.

2. Recognize progress and keep interest alive by being currently informed of what each of your immediate subordinates wants to do, can do, and is doing.

3. Represent each of your employees upstairs to your supervisor. Develop recognition plans to overcome the "they" complex.

4. Have informal discussion of performance, progress, and results. Try meeting at the other person's place of work or on neutral ground.

5. Face up to failures. Take early action to correct the causes.

6. Continually strive for higher standards of performance for yourself and for the individuals in your group. Keep yourself and your group improvement-minded and stretching toward definite and attainable objectives.

7. Set an example by your own performance and by your methods of managing.

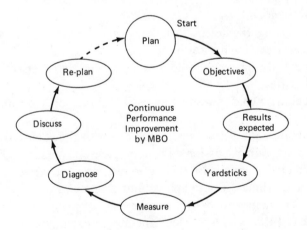

No one can make a *full* contribution to any organized effort unless:

1. They feel *enlisted* and *needed* in its improvement.
2. They *get* and *accept* invitations to assume a share of the success of the organization.

3. They see *their* performance as contributing to the organization's improvement and success.

SUMMARY

Internal negotiations inside the organization will most often be done on a one-on-one basis. By applying good negotiating techniques, your own personal affairs and career will be enhanced. There are more techniques such as TA, the problem-solving approach, and MBO which can be applied than are presently used.

In the following chapter are some cases and games which you can work on alone or with others in a training class or small-group negotiation development program.

15
Games and Cases for Practice in Negotiation Skills

> One must learn by doing the thing;
> for though you think you know it
> you have no certainty until you try.
> —Sophocles

In this chapter we'll present some practice in negotiation. In some instances you'll get the facts of a true case study with some of the details altered. In others you'll take part in a game in which you can make some strategic choices in dealing with another. Instructions for organizing a group of people in a class, seminar, or study group are included in each game or case.

THE GOLD AND SILVER GAME

This game illustrates how the strategy with which you play can affect your outcome. Here is how to organize the group.

1. Have the entire group of whatever size count off into threes. Starting, at the front of the room, each person calls a number "1-2-3," etc., until the entire group is divided into trios. Any extras become observers with other groups.

2. Now move into seated positions in which each trio can work without interference from the others. This can be done in the same room by grouping chairs, or people might use convenient lounges, cafeteria, etc.

Instructions

The number 1 players play Gold, number 2's play Silver, and number 3's are Observers. Each pair of Golds and Silvers plays the game eight times, after which their total scores are calculated and verified by the observer.

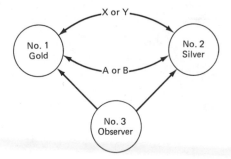

a. *Your objective:* To win more money than the other side in eight games. You do this by winning the biggest possible amount yourself while depriving the other side of possible winnings.

b. *Rules:* No talking between players except that the observer may talk to the players to verify their accounting.

Procedures for Play

a. Silver and Gold each tear a paper into four pieces. Silver writes "Silver" on his four papers, and Gold writes "Gold" on his.

b. Game 1 begins by Silver writing "X" or "Y" on a paper and passing it to Gold. Gold refers to the Value Table and writes "A" or "B" on the paper, records the number of dollars on his accounting sheet, and returns the paper to Silver, who records the dollars on his accounting sheet.

For example: If Silver chooses X, Gold may choose A, giving Silver +9 and Gold +9. If Gold chooses B, Silver gets −2 and Gold +16. If Silver chooses Y, Gold may choose A, giving Silver +10 and Gold −10. If he chooses B, he gives Silver −9 and Gold +9.

c. Game 2 begins by Gold writing "X" or "Y" on a slip and passing it to Silver. Silver writes "A" or "B" on that slip, records the scores, and returns the slip to Gold, who also records the scores.

d. Game 3 proceeds as game 1 above, and play continues for a total of 8 games, after which each player totals his net score, the sum of pluses minus the sum of minuses.

Value Table				Accounting		
		Silver	Gold	Game	S	G
Silver Use this table for games 1, 3, 5, 7	A	+9	+9		$	$
X	B	−2	+16			
Y	A	+10	−10	1/S		
	B	−9	+9	2/G 3/S		
Gold Use this table for games 2, 4, 6, 8	A	+9	+9	4/G		
X	B	+16	−2	5/S		
Y	A	−10	+10	6/G		
	B	+9	−9	7/S 8/G		
				Total	$	$
				Net: Sum of +'s less sum of −'s		

Rules for Observers

1. You are not to kibitz (help either Gold or Silver) but to watch carefully and be sure the rules of the game are followed. Warn the players against talking.

2. Be sure that Gold and Silver both have marked their four pieces of paper correctly.

3. After each transaction, check to be sure that each side has added and posted their scores correctly.

4. At the end, report to the parties your observations about the overall progress of the game and why you think the results came out as they did.

a. Who won the most?
b. Why?
c. Did the parties seem to get along, be angry, indifferent?
d. Any conclusions of a general nature about the game?

CASE NUMBER 1: THE NEW CAR CASE

The next case is long and contains three fairly extensive statements of the background and respective viewpoints of the two sides in the negotiation. The situation is that a young woman has an old car and wants to move up to a sports model new car. Once again, there are three roles:

Number 1 is the young woman buyer.
Number 2 is Dino the car salesman.
Number 3 is the observer.

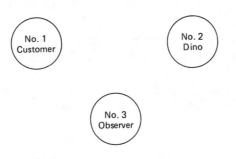

The objective: To get the maximum satisfaction for all sides through negotiation.

Instructions: Each person reads his or her own role carefully and makes notes, applying the factors in negotiation outlined in Chap. 5:

1. Construct a portfolio of your needs and wants.
2. Construct a portfolio of the other side's needs and wants.
3. Arrange a time and place to negotiate with the observer present.

This game requires careful reading in advance and some preparation before the meeting. If you are enrolled in a class in negotiation, make this a future class assignment.

RULES FOR PARTICIPANTS

Part I—Woman Customer

This is a true case reported by a student of one of the authors. She has experience as a purchasing agent.

Background: "The car I was driving, 'Tim,' a 1970 Plymouth Gold Duster, no longer fit the image I wanted to project, although he certainly met my other needs: reliable, roomy, easy to handle, good visibility, economical, and competitive on the road. Alas, poor Tim's appearance had become too conservative and so I decided to get rid of him. Tim's unacceptability didn't bloom overnight. It developed slowly. Seeds of doubt concerning Tim's appearance were planted by friends and family alike. Comments such as 'If I were footloose and fancy free like you I would drive a fancy sports car—not a box.' Another: 'If I had the money I would drive a nice little Triumph, Z, or MG.' A brother-in-law bent my ear every time I saw him about the virtues of the MG. I started noticing the sports cars on the road and in the foreign car lots. I started frequenting new car row comparing cars and sticker prices. The new car bug was thoroughly invading my body. A new job with an increased salary did the trick to win the battle for the new car bug. I was hooked. Now all I had to do was decide on the car for me and prepare for negotiations with whoever the lucky car salesman was to be."

Preparation: "I reviewed the sports car literature I had collected from the various dealers—looking at styling, performance characteristics, and sticker price plus price of options, plus I went to the library and read sports car journals. I discussed the various sports cars with friends and knowledgeable co-workers. I stopped by a couple of foreign car garages and spoke to the lead mechanic. I talked to my car insurance agent about cost of insurance. I called the Better Business Bureau and discussed various dealers and their service departments. I talked to my bank, other banks, and my credit union about financing. I took a test drive in the MGB, Porsche, Fiat, Triumph, and Mercedes 450 SEL. I narrowed my choice to the MGB, Fiat, or Triumph. The Porsche and Mercedes were out of my price range for this purchase—maybe next time. I finally decided on the MGB based on talks with the MG owners through the MG club, a friend's good experience with the MG, a co-worker's good experience, and finally my brother-in-law's enthusiastic support. I tentatively decided on a MG dealer based on talks with the

Better Business Bureau and talking to MG owners as they left that dealer's service department. Once I had decided on the dealer, I needed a salesman. I debated between the sales manager, the best salesman of the month, and the poorest salesman of the month. (It was nice of the dealer to post the salesmen's competition records for the public to see.)

"My preference was the sales manager as he was the one with authority to make a deal. However, I decided on the best salesman, who had a record to maintain. Prior to approaching the sales office, I sat down and made a list of the things I wanted:

Yellow MGB	Luggage rack
Overdrive	Black wall tires
Tonneau cover	Out-the-door price $4,600
AM/FM stereo radio	Dealer buy "Tim" for $1,500
Sport wheel covers	Total price $3,100 plus "Tim"

"According to bluebook, Tim's value was between $1,000 and $1,700. Tim was to be a separate transaction as far as the price of the MGB was concerned.

"Depending on interest charges, perhaps take dealer financing. My bank will finance cars for 12 percent, the credit union for 10 percent.

"I thought about my timing and decided to open negotiations toward the end of the month and just prior to the arrival of the next year's new line. I had noticed on one of my trips that the salesman had a selling contest going on that was to end July 31 and that this might play to my advantage.

"I decided to take a friend along to be my sports car expert. We discussed in advance that we should be enthusiastic about the MG as such but not overly sympathetic with the price: list at $5,500 including tax and license. I anticipated that the salesman would try to get me to finance the car through him and pay close to sticker price. Further that he would offer low bluebook for Tim. My opening position would be $1,800 for Tim as he was in such good condition and an out-the-door price for the MGB of $4,300. I would 'feel' the salesman out concerning the contest and what he would win in prestige and tangible goods. I would persuade him that his getting the car at the price I wanted would serve his needs too. As Tim was in good shape and had low mileage, I felt that I was in a good position with time on my side. There was no 'need' to rush into this deal."

Negotiation: "My friend and I arrived at the MG dealer after dinner one Wednesday evening toward the end of July. I decided on the best salesman, Dino, thinking that if Dino didn't respond properly, then I would talk to the manager or, if need be, go to another MG dealer. Dino was a friendly, smooth-talking salesman. We discussed the MG in general. I asked what he thought it would take to drive the car off the lot.

"Negotiate with Dino to get the best price possible for the yellow MGB."

Part II—Dino, MG Salesman

You are Dino, a new car salesman for a large, successful MG dealer. You have won the salesman of the year award for two consecutive years and are leading by a narrow margin in the contest which ends July 31 this year.

It is now July 24. It is near the year's production changeover and there is intensive promotion of this year's models, particularly the ones on the lots of the dealers. There is a green MGB, fully loaded, that has an extra $100 commission for the salesman if it is sold by July 31. It has overdrive, AM/FM radio, sport wheel covers, luggage rack, tonneau cover and many other sporty features. It lists at $5,500 including tax and license.

To get full commission on the green MGB plus the extra $100, you have to get the equivalent of $4,600. You will get extra commission if you can persuade the purchaser to finance and insure the car through the dealer. Of course you get extra commission also for each $100 over $4,600 you can negotiate on the sale of the MGB.

There is a yellow car available at another branch of the dealers similarly equipped listed at $5,500 but carrying no extra commission of $100.

A well-dressed woman enters the salesroom accompanied by a friend, asks for you, and indicates interest in a MGB. She is well informed about sports cars and MGBs.

She has a 1970 Gold Duster in very good condition and low mileage. The bluebook value of the Duster is $1,000–$1,700. Interest on dealer financing is 1½ percent a month.

You want to make the sale before July 31. You want to make as much commission as possible and also win the context.

She asks, "What would it take to drive a yellow MGB, equipped like that green one, off the lot?"

What do you reply?

Your objective is to sell her a car before July 31. How would you proceed?

> Your plan
> Timing
> Alternatives
> Combinations
> Opening price
> Final price

Role for Observer—Part III

The interested car buyer is described in Part I, Dino the MGB salesman in Part II. Part III is what happened in the actual situation and the observer's interpretations and comments on the negotiations:

1. What did the young woman do well?
2. What did Dino do well?
3. Comment on the planning
   > opening
   > concessions
   > strategy
   > timing
   > pricing
   > mutual interest
4. What could each negotiator learn from this bargaining?

What Actually Happened (for Observer Only)

"Dino felt he could get the manager to authorize a price of $5,200 with tax and license included—a $300 'savings'—as he had just sold one that afternoon for that price. He enthused about what a bargain $5,200 would be for that fine car. I told Dino that I thought he was a good salesman but that he would have to do better than that if we were going to do business. He asked me what I thought a 'fair' price would be. I told him that, based on the volume of cars sold, the base sticker price, and the end-of-a-season car, I thought $4,300 would be a reasonable price. He hesitated and before he could say anything my friend spoke

up and said that he thought $4,300 might be little too generous consid-
ering the infamous carburation problems with the MG plus the poor
grade of metal that the English use in the engine casting. Dino dropped
the price discussion and asked if I planned on financing the car myself
or through the dealer. He said he could get a good payment plan if I
wanted his financing—less than $100 per month with a final payment
of $343. I asked him what the interest rate was and he gave the monthly
rate, not annual. When I asked what the annual was, he said 'Eighteen.'
I told him he must be joking if he thought I would finance at 18 percent
when a commercial bank would lend at 12 percent and my credit union
would lend at 10 percent. I mentioned that it would be easier for us to
close a deal immediately if he would buy my car for $1,800. He and his
mechanic took Tim for a drive. After his drive he left my friend and me
and went to talk to his manager. When he came back he said that the
manager would be willing to approve a deal at $5,000 for the MG and
pay $1,100 for Tim. Dino also mentioned that the only MG with the
feature I wanted was a bottle green. I turned to my friend and said,
'Well, Tim has just received a reprieve.' I shook Dino's hand and
thanked him for his time and walked out. For some reason Dino looked
a little surprised. A couple of days later Dino called and said he could
get the yellow MG for a price of $4,900 and could probably give a little
more for the Plymouth. I told him $4,900 was still too much and my
car was worth $1,800. He said he didn't think he could get a better
price. We ended the phone call pleasantly. July 30 arrived as did a
phone call from Dino. He told me he had been thinking about me and
would like to discuss the MG a little further. I told him there wasn't
much point unless he was willing to sell for less than $4,900 and give
me a fair price for Tim. He asked me to stop by his office on my way
home that evening. I told him I would.

   "That evening Dino showed me the yellow MG and wanted me to
drive it, which I did. While I was driving it he talked to the manager
about price. When I got back he offered $1,250 for Tim and a selling
price of $4,750 for the MG. Dino mentioned that if he sold this car
tonight he would win the contest and get the trip to Mexico and win the
best salesman award for the third year in a row. I told Dino that I really
wanted the car and it would be neat if he won the contest and I would
be willing to accept $1,500 for Tim but would pay no more than $4,600
for the MG. Dino took the final figures and talked to the manager. Dino
came back and said $4,700 was rock bottom and $1,300 tops for my

car. I thanked Dino and told him that the most I would be willing to pay would be $3,100 cash plus my car and left. The next day—July 31—Dino called at lunch time and said if I could stop by before six p.m. with a check for $3,100 plus title to the Plymouth he could write up the deal and give me title to the yellow MG. I told him it was a deal. I signed the papers that night and drove home 'Myrn.' My credit union financed 'Myrn,' and the insurance agent was more than agreeable to insuring her. I was happy and so was Dino. He once again won salesman of the month and won the trip to Mexico. I think I was successful because I was prepared, had time, the dealer wanted to sell, and I did not allow myself to be pressured."

CASE NUMBER 2: A REAL ESTATE TRANSACTION

This is a shorter case which can be done right in class with the parties reading their roles immediately before playing the negotiation. Divide the class into three groups, two groups to prepare negotiation plans for the participants and the third to serve as observers.

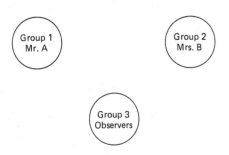

Objective: To negotiate a settlement which maximizes satisfaction to both sides.

Assignment: Groups 1 and 2 are to meet and devise plans for negotiation. Each side will prepare a *three-part price objective* with which it will enter bargaining, as below:

	Selling Price	*Buying Price*
Maximum	_____	_____
Realistic	_____	_____
Minimum	_____	_____

In other words, either side might be the buyer or the seller depending upon how the negotiations go. Using the above chart, list three levels of price for both buying and selling. Keep this confidential from the other side, of course, but provide a copy to the observer.

Instructions to Observers

1. You will receive a slip of paper from each side showing their minimum, realistic, and maximum buying prices, and also their minimum, realistic, and maximum selling prices. These must be kept confidential from the other party but should be used as a guide to your observations of how the negotiations develop.

2. *Observe and make notes of negotiations.* Note all offers, counteroffers, movements, and tactics employed. When the agreement is reached, you will report on the following:

a. What were the respective positions of the parties at the start of negotiations?

b. How did each approach the other?

c. Describe the ways negotiation developed. Remember you are acting as a *recorder* in negotiations.

d. What tactics did the parties use?

e. How effective were they?

NEGOTIATIONS FOR BUILDING ON A LOT

The situation: The following represents houses and vacant lots on a street in Ithaca, New York:

House	40-foot lot	60-foot lot	House
(Mrs. B's sister)	owned by B	owned by A	

Street

There are two adjoining vacant lots, one with 60-foot frontage and the other with 40-foot frontage. On each side of the lots are houses which were built five years ago. The 60-foot lot is owned by Mr. A and has a tax assessment value of $5,000. Mr. A purchased the lot ten years ago for $2,000. The adjoining lot is owned by Mrs. B who inherited it from her father ten years ago.

Present zoning laws require lots to have a minimum of 80-foot front-age for a single-family residence or a duplex home.

A similar lot with 80-foot frontage was sold two blocks away for $10,000 six months ago.

Both Mr. A and Mrs. B have an interest in acquiring the adjoining lot owned by the other. They have nearly equal financial resources.

Mrs. B's sister lives next door to the lot, and Mr. A lives several blocks away.

Instructions:

1. Break into three groups and develop your plans.
2. Conduct the negotiation.
3. At the end of negotiation, the observers report their critique to the entire group.

CASE NUMBER 3: R.S., THE NEW DIVISION CHIEF

Once again we divide the class into three groups:

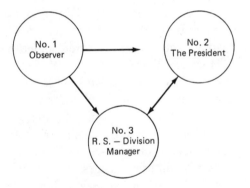

Your objective: To negotiate a settlement which maximizes gain for all concerned.

Suggested method: Apply the problem-solving system described in Chap. 14—"Head to Head—Negotiating on Your Own." Remember that a *problem is a deviation from an ideal or objective.*

1. Each side prepares a statement of the problem and lists some *optional courses* which could be tried.

2. Devise a plan for getting to your most desirable alternative.

3. Give a confidential copy of your *options* to the observer.

4. The observer will be the recorder and reporter on what happened in the negotiation and will offer comments on strategies, tactics, and different perceptions of the sides.

The situation follows, as related by the president:

"Last summer our company acquired a new division which opened a line of activities for us. Shortly thereafter, R.S. was hired to head this activity. During the ten months R.S. has worked for us, his results and performance have been outstanding. He has brought in a great deal of new business on a very profitable basis. As a result, the investment in this division has nearly been recovered from profits and we are facing the need to make an additional investment in plant expansion.

"When R.S. was originally hired, his last employer was contacted. He reported that R.S. had considerable ability and could be a valuable executive if some rather firm controls were applied which had been lacking in that company. Recently some information has come to our attention that R.S. had had difficulties in other places he had worked. As a result, a thorough check of his past record was made.

"The report discloses that in his last four positions R.S. had difficulties leading to his being discharged or asked to resign. His record shows that he has tremendous energy, ability, and ambition, but promises more than he can deliver and there are doubts about his integrity and strict honesty. In other companies he seems to start rapidly, get things going, and then becomes overly optimistic and sometimes misrepresents certain situations. However, there is no proof of dishonesty.

"R.S. is now fifty years of age. His work with us has been outstanding. We have no complaints, and we have no one to replace him. In fact we are dependent on him. We have no basis for discharging him except for information about his past record, which it now appears we should have found out before hiring him. If we did discharge him, he might very well ruin or take with him the business he has built up. If we retain him, we must go forward with our expansion plans, which of course are based on the business he is producing.

"R.S. may be making promises and deals of which we have no knowledge, using tactics with customers of which we would not approve and which in the long run will alienate them as he has done in the past, and may give our company a questionable reputation or even involve us in costly claims.

"We have not written an employment contract with R.S., but we have encouraged him to feel he has a fine future with the company. A settlement might be costly."

1. What should the president of the company do? The president's group takes three minutes to plan a discussion with R.S.

2. The group playing the role of R.S. takes three minutes to plan a discussion with the president. Then the leader asks the R.S. group to predict what the president will do in the negotiations and how they will react. Then the presidents are asked to present their plans, which might include some of the following notes:

"Can be good #2 person—not necessarily good #1 officer—50-year-olds change—can even get worse—old dogs can learn new tricks—may become old dogs."

CASE NUMBER 4: ALBERT SWANSON

This is another case of head-to-head bargaining, between Albert Swanson and a higher-level executive. The executive is two levels higher than Albert's boss. Divide into trios.

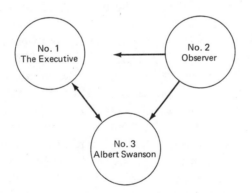

Objectives: To negotiate a settlement satisfactory to all concerned.

Method: Read the situation carefully, define the problem, and devise some optional solutions. Prepare a list of these options and submit a copy confidentially to the observer. Each side will plan its approach and conduct the negotiations.

The observer will be the recorder and reporter on what happened in negotiations.

At the end of the negotiations and report, ask each of the parties to explain their actions.

The Situation

Albert Swanson, age 39, is a managing engineer in the headquarters of an international oil company in New York City. He was transferred there fourteen months ago with a substantial increase in pay and received a generous merit raise two months ago.

Before coming to New York he had worked in the Midwest for this company since his graduation from the State University of Kansas seventeen years ago. For the seven years previous to the New York transfer he was regional engineer in Kansas City, his wife's home town. They have three children ages 12, 14, and 16. They live in a suburb 65 minutes commuting time from his New York office.

Two days ago a top executive of the company informed Albert that he was one of three candidates being considered for chief engineer of the worldwide company. The present chief is scheduled for retirement seven months from now. The company would like Albert to go to the Harvard Advanced Management Program for thirteen weeks. The course starts six weeks from now. The executive asks Albert if he has any questions before discussing the opportunity with Mrs. Swanson. What should Albert ask?

Mrs. Swanson was happier in Kansas City and would like to go back there. His former regional engineer job has been filled by an excellent manager 36 years of age who is doing a better job than Albert did.

Albert decides he would prefer to go back to Kansas City. He is tired of commuting. His family can live comfortably in Kansas City on the regional engineer's salary. They will own a very comfortable home there. The children are very interested in returning "home."

The next morning in an interview with the high executive, Albert thanks him for the opportunities but indicates he would like to go back to Kansas City and be the best regional engineer the company ever had.

1. How will the higher executive react to Albert's declining the job? What clichés can be expected? Does the executive still want Albert to go to Harvard and to be a candidate for chief engineer?

CASE NUMBER 5: PASSED OVER FOR THE PRESIDENCY

Frank had served six years as executive vice president. The president had informed him that he was being groomed for the presidency. He was given special assignments and tough projects, and had always done his work well. The president began spending more and more time in international business affairs, and that aspect of the business prospered, contributing most of the profit. A sudden health crisis caused the president to retire. Frank was designated acting president. One day the board of directors decided after three months that Frank did not have sufficient experience in the growing international field. They contacted a search outfit, which recommended a person from another firm. The board hired the new person as president. Frank is disappointed. He meets with the new president to clarify his future.

1. Break up into trio groups. One role is the new president, the other is Frank. The third is the observer.

2. Each side should devise a strategy and a plan of negotiation. Refer to the section in Chap. 14 on TA and choose a suitable ego state for yourself and your transactional strategy. What should you seek to play? To avoid?

3. The observer is the recorder and reporter.

RECOMMENDATIONS FOR FURTHER READING

As more of you become involved in negotiation, it will be of considerable importance that you keep studying and learning more. Not only are the techniques and skills of negotiation worth knowing, but the underlying theories and behavioral principles as well. The following list of suggested readings isn't exhaustive, but a sample of some of the best of the current writing on negotiation.

A few of them we have annotated with brief summaries, with the hope that a brief abstract might interest you in reading the entire volume.

1. Bacharach, Samuel, and Lawler, Edward J. *Bargaining: Power Tactics and Outcomes,* Jossey Bass, San Francisco, 1981.

A general theory of bargaining applicable to all sorts of negotiation, group or individual. Begins with a critique of what has been written to date, moves to the role of power in bargaining, how concessions occur, theories of deterrence and conflict spiral, how the parties punish one another, issue bluffs and arguments, and how power converges in bargaining. It concludes with a theory of bargaining power.

2. Cohen, Herbert. *You Can Negotiate Anything,* Lyle Stuart, New York, 1981.

This book is important for it was a general best seller in *The New York Times* top twenty books for over forty weeks. The reason is clear. Cohen is amusing and lucid and gives specific prescriptions about what to do and how to do it in negotiating. Not especially aimed at business but more of a personal, familiar, marital book, it is a goldmine of Machiavellian technique for winning.

3. Karrass, Chester. *Give and Take: The Complete Guide to Negotiating Strategies,* Thomas Y. Crowell Company, New York, 1974.

Karrass did his doctoral dissertation on negotiating and wrote a book in 1970 based upon that research, then came back in 1974 with this complete guide which is organized in an interesting and useful fashion as a reference guide. He takes all of the major subjects on negotiations from A to Z and catalogs them with handy references on how to cope with each topic. Easy to read, authoritative—a must for your library if you are going to do a lot of negotiating.

4. Fisher, Robert and Urey, William. *Getting to Yes,* New York, Penguin Books 1981.

This book is a product of a group in Cambridge called the Harvard Negotiation Project, written by a law professor and labor negotiator. It is rooted in *principle* being the basic mode to solution. Rather than figuring out what you want and then saying no to everything the other side asks for, try first to define your needs and their needs and then list options which might find unity between you. Their approach to conflict resolution is similar in many ways to the Kepner Tregoe problem-solving method: orderly and rational. They have little use for tricks and ploys, only principles.

5. Nirenberg, Gerard L. *Fundamentals of Negotiating,* Hawthorn Books, New York (3rd edition), 1973.

If you want to read the words of the father of modern negotiations, you read this one. Nirenberg got into negotiation as a generalized set of skills long before anyone else and made it a topic of popular interest and concern. He has several other related books, issues a negotiations newsletter, has recorded much of his thinking on audio tapes, and is director of a Negotiation Institute. A fountain of information, and for many, the person who taught America how to negotiate.

OTHER WORTHWHILE READING ON NEGOTIATION

Andree, Robert G. *The Art of Negotiation,* Heath Lexington Books, D. C. Heath and Company, Lexington, Massachusetts, 1971.

Coffin, Royce A. *The Negotiator: A Manual for Winners,* AMACOM, A division of American Management Association, New York, 1973.

Druckman, Daniel. *Negotiations: Social Psychological Perspective.* Sage Publications Inc., Beverly Hills, California, 1977.

Karrass, Chester L. *The Negotiating Game,* Thomas Y. Crowell, New York, 1970.

Snyder, William. *Negotiating Techniques,* Report 328, American Entrepreneurs Association, 1981

Young, Oran R. *Bargaining: Formal Theories of Negotiation,* University of Illinois Press, Urbana, 1975.

Footnotes

Chapter 1

1. Smith, Adam, *An Inquiry into the Nature and Causes of the Wealth of Nations.* E. Cannan, ed. New York: Random House, 1937.
2. Fiske, D., and Maddi, S. *The Functions of Varied Experience.* Homewood ILL: Dorsey Press, 1961.
3. *Strategic Planning for Human Resources.* Opinion Research Corporation, Princeton, 1981.
4. Marcuse, H. *One Dimensional Man.* Boston: Beacon Press, 1964.
5. Cron, R. L. *Assuring Customer Satisfaction,* New York: Van Nostrand Reinhold, 1979.

Chapter 3

1. Fisher, R., and Urey, W. *Getting to Yes.* New York: Penguin Books, 1981.

Chapter 4

1. Richardson, R. *Collective Bargaining by Objectives.* Housewood ILL: R. D. Irwin, 1975.

Chapter 6

1. French, J., and Raven, B. "The Bases of Social Power," in *Studies in Social Power.* Univ. of Michigan, 1959.
2. Siu, R. G. H. *The Craft of Power.* New York: John Wiley & Sons, 1979.

Chapter 7

1. Maccoby, M. *The GamesMan.* New York: Simon and Schuster, 1976.
2. Jennings, E. *Executive Stress.* Michigan State Univ. Press, 1974.

Chapter 8

1. Karass, C. *Give and Take.* New York: Thomas Y. Crowell, 1974.

Chapter 11

1. Cohen, H. *You Can Negotiate Anything.* New York: L. Stuart, 1979.

Chapter 12

1. Serrin, J. *The Company and the Union.* New York: A. Knopf, 1972.
2. Blake, R. *The New Managerial Grid.* Gulf Publishing, 1978.
3. Hare, A. *Handbook of Small Group Research.* Forel Press, 1962.

Chapter 13

1. Katz, Robert L. "Skills of an Effective Administrator," *Harvard Business Review* 74 (September–October 1974), 90–102.
2. Tactics, generally speaking, are airy ploys designed to distract the other party from real bottom-line issues. The leading book on tactics is Chester L. Karrass, *Give and Take* (New York: Crowell, 1974).
3. Ashok Kapoor, *Planning for International Business Negotiations,* (Cambridge, MA: Ballinger, 1975).

Chapter 14

1. Berne, E. *Games People Play*. New York: Ballantine, 1978.

Index